PROFILES IN CANADIAN DRAMA
GENERAL EDITOR: GERALDINE C. ANTHONY

Robertson Davies

PATRICIA MORLEY

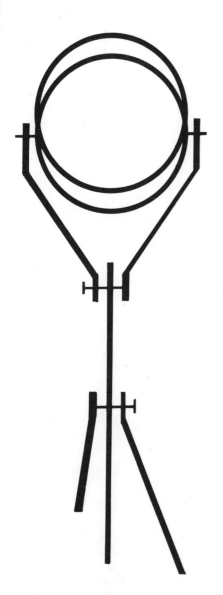

GAGE EDUCATIONAL
PUBLISHING LIMITED

Canadian Cataloguing in Publication Data

Morley, Patricia.
  Robertson Davies

  (Profiles in Canadian drama)

    Bibliography: p.
    Includes index.
    ISBN 0-7715-5874-0 bd.   ISBN 0-7715-5864-3 pa.
    1. Davies, Robertson, 1913-   - Criticism and
    interpretation.   I. Title.   II. Series
    PS8507.A95Z75   C812′.5′4   C76-017211-0
    PR9199.3.D3Z75

123456789 GL 84 83 82 81 80 79 78 77

Acknowledgements

We wish to thank the following for their co-operation and for their kind permission to quote copyrighted material:

Mr. Robertson Davies for assistance to the author in preparation of the manuscript and for permission to quote from "Leaven of Malice" © Robertson Davies, 1973 and "Brothers in the Black Art" © Robertson Davies, 1974.

Clark, Irwin & Company Limited, Toronto, and Robertson Davies for permission to quote from Robertson Davies: *A Jig for the Gypsy* © 1954, *At the Gates of the Righteous* © 1949, *A Masque of Aesop* © 1952, *At My Heart's Core* © 1950, *Voice of the People* © 1949, *Hope Deferred* © 1949, *Fortune My Foe* © 1949, *Eros At Breakfast* © 1949.

The Macmillan Company of Canada Limited, Toronto, for permission to quote from Robertson Davies: *A Mixture of Frailties* © 1958, 1968 and Donald Cameron: *Conversations with Canadian Novelists* © 1973.

New Press, Toronto, for permission to quote from Robertson Davies: *General Confession* © 1972, *Hunting Stuart* © 1972, and *King Phoenix* © 1972.

Oxford University Press Canada, Toronto, for permission to quote from Robertson Davies: *A Masque of Mr. Punch* © 1963.

Preface

"Profiles in Canadian Drama" is a series of books on Canadian dramatists launched in 1976 with the intention of presenting to Canadians on a regular basis, books on individual Canadian playwrights, both English and French. As the series progresses it is hoped that a fairly comprehensive picture of Canada will emerge, since these analytical studies should cover every region, temperament, tone and personality of our country. From the complexity of social views expressed, the range of characters depicted, and the responses to life revealed, there should gradually emerge a mosaic that, seen in its entirety, may surely be called Canada. Even more telling will be the *pentimento* effect of seeing layer upon layer of life delineated as one approaches the primary portrait.

The first four books in the series represent highly differentiated studies in contrast. *Gratien Gélinas* by Renate Usmiani seeks to present a picture of French Canada through the plays of Gélinas whose works faithfully record the evolution of French Canadians from narrow provincialism to sophisticated individualism. *James Reaney* by J. Stewart Reaney aims at a clarification of the role that 'family' plays in the dramas of rural Perth County, Ontario, in a deliberate rejection of city. *George Ryga* by Gerald McCaughey emphasizes the aspect of social criticism in Ryga's plays on the plight of the Indian in Canada today. The present volume *Robertson Davies* by Patricia Morley observes Davies' preoccupation with middle-class Canadian pretensions in the Shavian style of irony and satire. Robertson Davies, urbane, sophisticated Canadian novelist, has experimented successfully with drama in producing seventeen plays which, observed as a whole, may be said to depict the Davies view of middle-class Canada. Called by some critics the George Bernard Shaw of Canadian theatre, Davies has put his cultivated taste and critical insight to work in order to produce an ironic view of Canadian life that is at the same time manifestly true.

Dr. Morley has given a perceptive and clear overall survey of the total Davies body of dramatic work. Herself a native of Ontario and author of books on Canadian writers, Dr. Morley, has concentrated her energies within the critical area of Canadian Literature. Her study of Robertson Davies' plays emphasizes the tension between his romantic and his ironic points of view. A satirist of Canadian anti-intellectualism and materialism, he is also a romantic idealist dependent on feeling and intuition. He draws his material from his own experiences as a member of an upper middle-class family, a newspaper editor, and a professor of drama. His themes revolve around a hatred of pretension and cant as he examines romantic love, honor, beauty, life and freedom within the framework of pretentious middle-class Canadian families. Davies' philosophy of inner peace and self-knowledge is evidenced in his preoccupation with Jung's analytical psychology. As a result he examines Jungian concepts in his plays: *General Confession, Hunting Stuart,* and *Question Time.* Davies' work also reflects his absorption in music, song and spectacle, particularly in his use of Jonson's anti-masque, a comic interlude parodying the masque's main plot, which he uses to advantage in two of his own masques. Dr. Morley remarks upon Davies' justification of the use of melodrama in social criticism, as well as his sense of theatricality in fashioning his plays. His comic vision stemming from his religious faith, and his understanding of myth proceeding from his perception of religious ritual support a drama that joins humor with mystery in its efforts to explore the Canadian conscience.

Patricia Morley sees Robertson Davies' place in the development of a national Canadian drama as that of the satirist. This brief study should appeal to the general public as well as those directly connected with theatre — actors, directors, producers. Written primarily for university and secondary school students, their professors and teachers, it should however serve to involve all its readers in Canadian theatre as a national mirror.

Geraldine Anthony, S.C.
Mount Saint Vincent University
Halifax, Nova Scotia

Contents

CHAPTER

1 The Entertainer 1

2 Marchbanks' Doppelganger 7

3 Don Quixote and the Philistines 12

4 The Guise of Beauty 26

5 Davies' Masques 42

6 'The Comedy Company of the Psyche' 50

7 'Through scorn, to love' 65

Bibliography 69

Index 72

1

The Entertainer

Davies' fictional magician Eisengrim, in *Fifth Business*, is a man who offers entertainments "of mystery and beauty, with perhaps a hint of terror as well." This description might well be applied to Davies' own work. Most of Davies' drama is romantic comedy but (again like Eisengrim) he is not simply a funny-man. On the one hand Davies is a romantic idealist; on the other, he is a satirist with a sharp eye for human foibles and folly and a witty tongue to express what he sees. Davies' style is the result of the tension between his romantic and ironic points of view. Interestingly, Davies defines humour, in his essay on Leacock, as a result of tension in the mind.[1]

Much of his satire is at the expense of Canadian intellectualism and Canadian materialism. The Philistines, in the Old Testament, were the enemies of God's people, the Israelites. Matthew Arnold applied the term to materialists who do not appreciate art and the things of the spirit. Davies' satirical thrusts express his love for Canada, since he believes that no nation can be great without cultivating the arts.

Eros at Breakfast, one of his earliest plays, is full of sly digs at Canadians as rationalists who are really anti-intellectuals. Most of the bureaucrats in charge of Mr. P.S.'s internal system believe that lovers (like blonds) have more fun, but the head of the Intelligence Department declares that a Canadian's Intelligence is a curb upon his baser instincts. Mr. P.S.'s professors are described as a considerate lot who keep thinking down to a minimum. Mr. P.S. himself is a typical young Canadian with no tiresome intellectual curiosity of any sort. His Solar Plexus plays no part in his poetry, which is squeezed out painfully by his Intelligence Department.

Davies describes the theatre as a temple of feeling, a temple "where dreams and wishes are paramount, and where prophecies are made."[2] His plays also have a sizeable intellectual component, something which the playwright is quick to deny in conversation. He has described his plays as being "all about emotion," adding that he does not believe in intellectual theatre: "Unless the theatre excites people and makes them laugh or weep, it's missing its function."[3]

The description of the theatre as a temple where wishes and dreams are uppermost points to drama as a method of psychic exploration rather than as a social mirror. Davies' drama serves both functions but moves, through the forties and fifties, from a more external to a more internal focus. His early interest in Freudian psychoanalytic theory, and his increasing interest in the writings of Carl Jung, directed this movement. His plays move from the relatively simplistic idea of the multiplicity of the human personality found in *Eros at Breakfast* to the sophisticated Jungian concepts which underlie *Hunting Stuart* and *General Confession*.

The Jungian theory of human personality is explored at length in his novel *The Manticore*, where the hero David Staunton is a man of over-developed intellect and under-developed feeling. Davies describes himself as the opposite kind of person. He is not, he claims, a very good thinker, and is "scrappily" educated: "In Jungian terms I am a feeling person with strong intuition. I *can* think, I've *had* to think, and I *do* think, but thinking isn't the first way I approach any problem . . . . I get it through my fingertips, not through my brain . . . . Also intuition is very strong in me; I sort of smell things."[4]

Davies' love of music is evident in everything he writes. Most of his plays include a song, a dance, or both, and music also plays an important part in his novels. The title of his best-known novel, *Fifth Business*, is taken from an operatic term. In his second book on the Shakespearean Festival at Stratford, Davies praises Tyrone Guthrie's musical sensibility which becomes, as Guthrie directs, a sure sense of dramatic rhythm. He quotes Bernard Shaw, that there is a musical counterpart for much of what happens in all plays of classical stature. Davies structures *Eros at Breakfast*, for example, around Prokofiev's *Classical Symphony*. Prokofiev is the hero's favorite composer. The symphony introduces the various scenes, while a Strauss waltz (preferably, according to the directions, "The Thousand and One Nights") is used to suggest the personality of Parmenes, representative of the Heart. In "Leaven of Malice," the pace and mood of the various parts of the dream sequence are described in musical terms. The sense of rhythm which he ascribes to Guthrie's direction is evident in the best of Davies' drama.

The truth of art is expressed through symbol and myth. Ritual is the enactment of myth, and theatre has developed from religious ritual. Davies is very conscious of this, and also of the psychoanalytic interpretation of ritual as something which dredges up from the depths of memory a primary human experience which is normally repressed.[5] Tyrone Guthrie, in the concluding essay of the book written by Davies and himself on the 1954 Stratford Shakespearean Festival, describes theatre as making its effect not by illusion or imitation but by ritual or symbolic re-enactment. Theatre, Guthrie writes, is the direct descendant of "all the corporate ritual expressions by means of which our primitive ancestors, often wiser than their progeny, sought to relate themselves to God, or the gods, the great abstract forces, which cannot be apprehended by reason; but in whose existence reason compels us to believe."[6]

When asked whether his comic vision was connected to his religious faith, Davies said, yes, the two are inextricable.[7] He holds that gloom is self-indulgent. The idealistic and mystical side of his vision comes through in a remark like Chremes' injunction to the audience in *Eros at Breakfast*: "All life is miraculous."

His prolific output of drama and fiction, despite the many other demands on his time, is the result of self-discipline (an ideal promoted in more than one of his works) and a puritan work schedule of seventy hours a week or more. Davies might not care for the word *puritan* but I have tried, elsewhere, to redeem it from the exclusively pejorative usage of our generation.[8] He writes quickly, rarely for more than half an hour at a time; revises at great length; and carries a notebook in which to record ideas. Bernard Shaw said that man is a creature of habit: one does not write three plays and then stop. Davies "habit" of writing had been firmly established by the end of the forties.

His versatility and range are apparent from the briefest survey of his work. Settings in his plays vary from contemporary Canada to twelfth-century Britain. He has published fourteen plays: five one-acters, in *Eros at Breakfast and Other Plays*(1949); two masques (1952 and 1963); seven full length plays: *Fortune, My Foe*(1949), *At My Heart's Core*(1950), *A Jig for the Gypsy*(1954), and *Hunting Stuart and Other Plays*(1972), which contains *King Phoenix* and *General Confession* along with the title play. And *Question Time*, a Jungian fantasy premiered at the O'Keefe Centre in February 1975 and published later that year. Three further full-length plays have not yet been published. "Leaven of Malice," a dramatic version of his 1954 novel by the same name, was performed at Toronto's Hart House Theatre in 1973. "Brothers in the Black Art"(1974) is a romantic comedy for television. "The Centennial Play"(1966, 1967) was written in collaboration with four other playwrights in honor of Canada's hundredth birthday. It was coordinated by Davies.

"The Centennial Play" is a review of Canada from five different points of view, a glimpse of five regions by five authors, one each from the Maritimes (Arthur Murphy), Quebec (Yves Theriault), Ontario (Robertson Davies), the Prairies (W.O.Mitchell), and British Columbia (Eric Nicol). It was successfully performed in Lindsay in 1966, supervised by Leon Major. Davies dissociates himself from the 1967 production in Ottawa revised and directed by Peter Boretski.

The Ontario scene depicts a primary school on Inspection Day. It is amusing light comedy, suited to the review style. Davies gets in a few digs at English-Canadian complexes such as learning the names of the Kings of England instead of the Prime Ministers of Canada, believing that alcohol is the root of all evil, and that the highest art instils only moral conduct. The five skits are held together by two actors called Nanabozho and Fox. The latter is a shrewd and energetic godling who represents that part of the country which is for material things and greed. Nanabozho is described as representing the spirit (sometimes dormant) of Canada: ''He has given up on Canada and as the play progresses his faith and spirit about the country are rejuvenated.'' The review form has always been popular in Canada: witness the continuing popularity of *Spring Thaw* and the wild triumph of *My Fur Lady*.

Davies' critical writings on drama include *Shakespeare's Boy Actors*, originally his Oxford thesis, *Shakespeare for Young Players*, numerous articles, and three works in collaboration with Sir Tyrone Guthrie on the Shakespeare Festival at Stratford, Ontario: *Renown at Stratford* (1953); *Twice Have the Trumpets Sounded* (1954); and *Thrice the Brinded Cat Hath Mew'd* (1955). This is criticism at its best: witty, urbane, and gracious. There is nothing of the scholarly pedant in Davies, and this type is often the butt of his wit.

He is as well known for his fiction as for his drama, and the student of his plays will find that light is cast on these works by the fiction, which is not surprising. Davis likes to do things by threes. There are three Marchbanks books, collections of witty comments by the fictional Samuel Marchbanks. Davies' novels of the fifties are commonly called the Salterton trilogy, because of their setting in the university town of Salterton, alias Kingston. They are *Tempest-Tost* (1951), *Leaven of Malice* (1954), and *A Mixture of Frailties* (1958). The three novels in the Salterton trilogy have a loosely sequential plot. A religious mythology, and a movement from bondage towards freedom, underlies the entire trilogy. More recently, Davies has published *Fifth Business* (1970), *The Manticore* (1972), and *World of Wonders* (1975). This trilogy is strongly influenced by Jungian ideas and may be related to *Hunting Stuart*, *General Confession*, and *Question Time*, the most Jungian of the plays.

What of Davies' place in the development of a national drama? It is difficult to assess in so short a space and while we are still so close to the period in time. But clearly his plays made an important contribution to the flowering of an indigenous drama in the first ten years after the Second World War. Davies also encouraged the Stratford venture as one of the Board of Governors of the Festival Theatre and through his books, with Guthrie, in its critical first three years. The Shakespearean Festival has given Canadian actors, stage-designers, producers and, latterly, dramatists, new opportunities, and the Canadian public its first look at theatrical excellence of the highest order.

Modern comedy tends largely to three types: black comedy, with its gallows humour and its revelation of the disorder of existence; satire; and sentimental comedy. Tragedy, Davies believes, is incompatible with democracy, for the tragic hero should be, in Sir Philip Sidney's phrase, a ''high fellow,'' a man upon whom the fate of many others depends. The temper of our age is anti-heroic. Comedy is the prevailing mode, and this is especially true in Canada.[9]

Davies hates sentimentality. The special quality of his comedies lies in their being romantic without being sentimental, or romantic and satiric at once. Davies regards romance as a quality inherent in comedy, and professes to be astonished by the naïveté and thinness of what many people call romance.[10] In *Fifth Business*, Dunstan Ramsay speculates on people's need for marvels, a need which arises out of some deep knowledge that *the marvellous is really an aspect of the real*. The irrational will have its say, he thinks, "perhaps because 'irrational' is the wrong word for it." Davies' comedies stand out from the mass by their ability to project something "marvellous" or mysterious, the quality he calls *romance*.

A country with a scattered population spread over a vast territory is not a fertile field for the development of a professional theatre. Native plays in the late nineteenth century tended to be written for reading rather than production, like Heavysege's *Saul* and Charles Mair's *Tecumseh*, while professional theatres were too expensive for anything but touring companies from Britain and the United States. Hart House Theatre had been donated to the University of Toronto by the Massey family in 1919. Little Theatre, or community theatre groups, had flourished between the two World Wars. The bilingual Dominion Drama Festival, founded in 1932, and various one-act play competitions had encouraged the production of short plays. Neither the Depression of the thirties nor the Second World War were circumstances in which the theatre could thrive. But shortly after the war things began happening, especially in Toronto, the centre of the performing arts in English-language Canada.

In an astringent article which ends in a biting attack on the Stratford Festival, Nathan Cohen sketches the development of post-war theatre in English Canada.[11] He begins by saying that serious theatre has never counted in the life of English-speaking Canadians, nor is it likely to in the near future — a prophecy which did not anticipate the rapid growth of festivals and permanent new theatres in the sixties and seventies. Cohen notes a sharp increase in theatrical activity between 1946-58, especially in Toronto. In 1947 Mrs. Dora Mavor Moore and her son Mavor set up the New Play Society, using the concert hall of the Royal Ontario Museum. The settings were makeshift, the directing and acting inexperienced, but the company's enthusiasm and sense of mission drew loyal audiences from the start. In the same year Hart House Theatre acquired a full-time director who was to put on four shows a year with student personnel. In 1949 the International Players of Kingston gambled with Davies' *Fortune, My Foe*, and it was an instant success. All of these groups were searching for a drama and a style of production upon which they could put their own stamp. The early fifties saw the establishment of the Crest Theatre in Toronto by the Davis brothers, and, of course, Stratford. Directed first by Tyrone Guthrie and later by Michael Langham, it has helped to raise theatre standards across Canada. Davies had no connection with the New Play Society, but several of his plays were written for Crest productions.

The language in Davies' work is robust, sometimes Rabelaisian. He has a marked antipathy to cant. He loves music, genuine spectacle, and mystery. He has a romantic fascination with myth, and a feeling for its religious truth. His drama joins pathos, humor, satire, even farce, to beauty and grandeur. His best plays — and here I would include *Fortune, My Foe*, "Leaven of Malice," *Hunting Stuart*, and *General Confession* — are steps in Canada's progress towards a drama which will take its place, like some of our fiction of the last ten or fifteen years, among the classics of world literature.

Notes to Chapter 1

1. See C.T.Bissell, ed., *Our Living Tradition: Seven Canadians* (Toronto: University of Toronto Press, 1957), p.129.

2. Robertson Davies, "The Theatre," in D.C.Williams, ed., *The Arts as Communication* (Toronto: University of Toronto Press, 1962), p.22.

3. Conversation at Massey College, 20 August 1974.

4. Donald Cameron, *Conversations with Canadian Novelists*, Part I (Toronto: Macmillan, 1973), p.42. There is an interesting parallel between Davies "scrappy" education and that of Ben Jonson, an English dramatist whom Davies acknowledges as an influence on his work. Although considered to be the most learned of the Elizabethan dramatists, Jonson's formal education was limited to a few years at Westminster School.

5. See Robertson Davies and Tyrone Guthrie, *Twice Have the Trumpets Sounded* (Toronto: Clarke, Irwin, 1954), p.130.

6. Ibid., p.193.

7. Conversation, 20 August 1974. Davies is a member of the Anglican Church, but said he felt an affinity with Orthodox Churches (Greek and Russian) because their understanding of evil is more profound than that of the Protestant churches. His father is a Presbyterian. Davies thinks of Presbyterianism as a non-sacramental faith, "a teaching rather than a feeling church."

8. See Patricia Morley, *The Immoral Moralists:Hugh MacLennan and Leonard Cohen* (Toronto:Clarke, Irwin, 1972). In conversation, Davies agreed that the word *puritan* implies a discipline, something very necessary to the production of art.

9. Cf. William Solly, "Nothing Sacred: Humour in Canadian Drama in English," *Canadian Literature*, 11 (Winter, 1962), 15: "Humour occupies an important place in Canadian drama in English, and most of our plays—and nearly all our best plays—rely heavily upon it." I consider Davies', and Sir Philip Sidney's, classic definition of tragedy to be narrow, and not necessarily definitive.

10. Conversation, 20 August 1974.

11. Nathan Cohen, "Theatre Today: English Canada," *Tamarack Review*, 13 (Autumn, 1959), pp.24-37. An article by Jean Hamelin on contemporary French-Canadian drama follows.

2

Marchbanks' Doppelganger

The wittiest if not the definitive biography of Robertson Davies has been written by Samuel Marchbanks, Davies' double.[1] Marchbanks' irascible temperament, however, leads him into some uncharitable observations which it is the duty of a more objective biographer to redress.

Davies is Canadian-born, of Welsh, Scottish and Dutch ancestry. On his father's side he is Welsh, with a small dash of Scottish blood. His mother's maternal forbears came to this continent from Holland in the eighteenth century, and to Canada at the time of the American Revolution. Her father was a Highland Scot. Asked whether he felt that his Celtic ancestry was the dominant strain, Davies replied that his mother was a very imaginative woman and that the Dutch are not without imagination. In his Introduction to *Eros at Breakfast*(1949), Tyrone Guthrie writes that both of Davies' parents made an impression of quite extraordinary force: "The grapple, largely but not wholly unconscious, with The Family patently underlies many of the ideas that emerge in these plays — notably it governs the concept of 'Canada,' dear and formidable."

Davies was born in Western Ontario in the village of Thamesville on August 28, 1913 a birthday he is proud of sharing with Goethe and Tolstoy. He is the third and youngest son of Florence (Mackay) and William Rupert Davies, later Senator. His father controlled the Thamesville *Herald*. His successes in publishing and in other business ventures permitted his son to be educated at Upper Canada College and later at Queen's University and at Oxford.

Marchbanks tells us that Davies' childhood was uneventful. He had neither a Durable Early Sorrow, a traumatic instance of Injustice, nor a single sign of Superior Aesthetic Perception. He liked school, stood near the top of his class, and was (not surprisingly) very fond of reading.

The unusual feature of his career at Upper Canada College (1928-1932) was his weakness in mathematics. Marchbanks, with his usual acerbity, calls him

The Mathematical Moron.[2] Since the matriculation regulations of 1932 required all students to pass mathematics, Davies failed to qualify for university entrance in Canada. He was permitted to attend Queen's as a "special student"; he read, and had no trouble passing, examinations which did not involve mathematics. This was followed by three years at Balliol College, Oxford, where he received the degree of B.Litt. in 1938 for a thesis written about boy actors in Shakespeare's theatre.

Another feature of his early education was his interest in music. He had played the piano since he was eight, but at U.C.C. his enthusiasm was directed towards music in a wider sense. Davies describes himself as a bad but enthusiastic pianist and singer, a man who drags music into everything he does. He says that music influenced his writing in the way that it influenced the writing of James Joyce: "I'm always thinking in musical terms and there are various devices which are common in symphonic music that are transferable to the novel. One of them is the disappointed climax. . . . You lead people right up to some extraordinary expectation, then cut it off . . . . You leave it to them to complete what has to be said, or heard."[3]

His passion for the theatre dates from childhood. He first appeared in public at the age of three in the Ferguson Opera House, Thamesville, as part of a chorus of children in the opera *Queen Esther*.[4] He saw a Punch and Judy show when he was a child, and made model theatres and puppets—not well, he says, because a of a lack of manual dexterity. Puppets play a role in *A Masque of Mr. Punch* (1963), and in *Fortune, My Foe* (1949), where the artistry of Szabo's Bohemian Puppets is responsible for persuading Nicholas Hayward to decide to stay in Canada. The first stage show Davies remembers seeing was a melodrama by the Marks family. Maybelle Marks sang patriotic songs between the acts (this was during the First World War) and Davies remembers being impressed by the combination of song and drama. His parents were interested in theatre, and his father acted in amateur productions. Davies himself was frequently in plays and in Gilbert and Sullivan operettas, both as a schoolboy and during his years at Queen's University.

At Oxford, Davies was stage manager for the Oxford University Dramatic Society. After graduation, he looked for work in the theatre. He obtained an acting tour with a provincial company, then a job at the Old Vic Repertory Company, London, as actor and as lecturer, in the school maintained by the Old Vic, on the history of theatre. He enjoyed two seasons with this famous old company (1938-40) and with director Tyrone Guthrie before the Second World War closed the theatres. In February 1940, Davies married Australian-born Brenda Mathews, stage manager of the Old Vic, and returned to Canada, where he was rejected for war service and began a career in editing and publishing. When asked recently what first led him to become a writer Davies replied: "Nothing led me to becoming a writer. I was born a writer the way the son of a chimney sweeper is born to be a chimney sweeper. My father was a writer. Both my brothers wrote things. I had a great uncle who was quite a remarkable writer. I had another great uncle who was a quite eminent medical writer, and writing just ran in the family.''[5]

He became book reviewer and literary editor of *Saturday Night* (1940-42), then editor of the *Peterborough Examiner* (1942-62). His long experience in newspaper work forms the basis of his play ''Brothers in the Black Art'' and of both the novel and the play ''Leaven of Malice''. It was in the columns of the *Examiner* that Davies' alter ego, Samuel Marchbanks, was born. Selections from his newspaper columns were published as *The Diary of Samuel Marchbanks*(1947), *The Table Talk of Samuel Marchbanks*(1949), and *Samuel Marchbanks' Almanack*(1967). In his essay on Davies, Marchbanks describes himself as follows: ''My life has been stormy, for there is nothing I like better than contradicting people and shouting them down. I am rude on principle, for there are too many boobs in the world who trade on the politeness of others in order to air their own ineptitude. I like to go among people and mock and jeer. I am anti-social, but I like society.''[6] Marchbanks, native of Skunk's Misery, Ontario, expresses Davies' satiric and Swiftian side. Every man is many men, as Davies, and Jung, are constantly reminding us. Marchbanks' witty, anarchic and acidic voice is one of the voices that sounds through Davies' Drama.

Davies told Donald Cameron that wit is a defensive mechanism. It diverts enemies from one's trail. ''I think I am concealing a painful sensitivity, because I am very easily hurt . . . .''[7] He discovered early in life, like Dunstan Ramsay in *Fifth Business*, the defensive value in ''getting off a good one.'' Wit is also generated as a reaction to narrowness, meanness, and want of charity. Such situations, and people, inevitably provoke hyperbole: ''It comes out in terms of savage, bitter humour, just because you don't quite want to go to savage denunciation, but you want to blast them like an Old Testament prophet. Instead you just swat them around with the jester's bladder.''[8] If you blasted them like a prophet, Davies adds, they might forgive you; if you mock them like a jester, they never will.

Since 1960, Davies has taught English at the University of Toronto (Chancellor Professor at Trinity College in 1960-61; at Trinity and University College in 1961-62; and from 1962 on, at University College). In 1962 he was appointed the first Master of Massey College, a post he continues to hold. He took up his duties when the new college for post-graduate work opened in September 1963. In 1964 he was appointed Edgar Stone Lecturer in Dramatic Literature. In cooperation with Professor Clifford Leech in the late sixties, Davies established the Drama Centre for graduate work within the University of Toronto. His time is currently divided between academic administration and the teaching of drama.

In *Fortune, My Foe*, Professor Rowlands says that teaching means forever going back to the beginning, whereas an artist must press on. In his own life, Davies enjoys teaching. You *do* go back to the beginning, he says, but not with the same people. The symbiotic relationship between teacher and student means that the teaching is always new.

Davies' numerous honours and awards include the Barry Jackson award for *Fortune, My Foe* and the Louis Jouvet prize for directing *The Taming of the Shrew*, both from the Dominion Drama Festival, 1949; the Leacock medal for humour for *Leaven of Malice*, 1955; the Lorne Pierce medal for contribution to Canadian literature, 1961; and the Governor General's Award for Fiction for *The Manticore*, 1973. He was made a Fellow of the Royal Society of Canada in 1967, a Companion of the Order of Canada in 1972, and holds honorary doctorates from no less than ten Canadian universities. Not a bad record for a man who describes himself as "scrappily" educated.

Davies is still writing plays, but in the last fifteen or twenty years, more of his artistic energy has gone into fiction. As he told Peter Sypnowich in 1971, some ideas demand to be treated as drama; others, as fiction.[9] The vision behind both is the same, and that vision is basically religious. Davies sees man as a creature both noble and ridiculous. His idealism is contained by a tremendous sense of humour.

He is a man of many talents: actor, drama teacher, novelist, humorist, critic, publisher, journalist, and academic administrator. But Marchbanks' laconic description—"he writes plays"—best sums up the man we are concerned with here.

Notes to Chapter 2

1. See Samuel Marchbanks, pseud. for Robertson Davies, "The Double Life of Robertson Davies," Carl F. Klinck and Reginald Watters,eds., *Canadian Anthology*, rev. ed. (Toronto: Gage,1966), pp.393-400.

2. It is curious that a man without any mathematical sense should be able to so quickly and accurately assess the cost of psychoanalysis to rid himself of a Doppelganger Delusion, an obsession caused by his resemblance to one Samuel Marchbanks, well known creator of jewelled prose. See Marchbanks, "The Double Life of Robertson Davies," pp.394-399.

3. "Acta Interviews Robertson Davies," *Acta Victoriana*, Vol. XCVII, No. 2 (April, 1973), p.81.

4. See Murray Edwards, *A Stage in our Past* (Toronto: University of Toronto Press, 1968), for a picture of the small but elegant Ferguson Opera House in Thamesville where Davies made his acting debut.

5. *Acta Victoriana*, p.72.

6. See Marchbanks, "The Double Life of Robertson Davies," p.398.

7. Donald Cameron, *Conversations with Canadian Novelists*, Part I (Toronto:Macmillan,1973), p.42.

Cf. James Strachey,ed., *The Standard Edition of the Complete Psychological Works of Sigmund Freud*, trans. J.Strachey, Vol.5 (London:Hogarth Press,1958), p.530. Speaking of verbal ambiguity, jokes, etc., Freud writes: "Whenever one psychical element is linked with another by an objectionable or superficial association, there is also a legitimate and deeper link between them which is subjected to the resistance of the censorship."

8. Cameron, *Conversations*, p.43.

9. See Peter Sypnowich, "Toronto author: writers shouldn't write for money," *Toronto Daily Star*, 23 Jan.1971, where Davies describes the whole theatre business as "very chancy. . . . There is also the fact, too, that when you write a novel even if a publisher refuses it or doesn't like it you have a very pleasant relationship with him. In the theatre the relationships are so extraordinarily difficult—not unpleasant, but demanding, and extreme—that you get less anxious about that as you get older, unless you have enjoyed a great deal more success than I have."

3

Don Quixote and the Philistines

The recurring theme in Davies' early drama, product of the late forties, is the state of cultural malnutrition which prevails in his land. In *A Mixture of Frailties*, the last of the Salterton trilogy of novels, the Gall family illustrate the problem. Monica Gall, the young singer who is redeemed from the "musical hell" of the Heart and Hope Gospel Quartet, is described by an English conductor as having "lived for twenty years in circumstances which are not discouraging to art—we see plenty of that—but in which art in any of its forms is not even guessed at." Monica, it is stressed, is very like her mother. Old Ma Gall, with her jokes, her tall stories and her keen insight, is a spoiled artist, "one who had never made anything, who was unaware of the nature or genesis of her own discontent, but who nevertheless possessed the artist's temperament; in her that temperament, misunderstood, denied and gone sour, had become a poison which had turned against the very sources of life itself."[1]

Ma and Monica Gall are Davies' images of Canada's cultural past and glowing future, the lost opportunities and the exciting potential which the present generation is beginning to exploit. Monica is determined that what was best in her mother should live on, and find expression, in her. *Fortune My Foe, Hope Deferred, The Voice of the People, Overlaid,* and *At My Heart's Core* dramatize Canada's past neglect of art. The former also expresses Davies' faith in the new generation to repair the sins of omission of the older ones. As Mavor Moore notes, Davies was tackling in his own way "the root questions of home, family and identity as they were posed by the times."[2]

Fortune, My Foe, is Davies' first three-act play. It was written in a hurry at the request of Arthur Sutherland for his summer theatre in Kingston, and has had frequent performances in Canada since 1949. In the preface to the 1968 reprint, Davies describes the theme as somewhat outdated, since conditions for artists and intellectuals have greatly improved since the forties. But he considers Nicholas' final speech, concerning the challenge of living in Canada, to be as relevant as when it was first written. Canada, Nicholas says, is a hard country to live in, but if everyone runs away it will never improve: "'let Canada do what she will with us, we must stay.'' Davies himself is not a man to run away from a challenge. A lively sense of nationality, and a sense of love and obligation towards one's country, is actually a very contemporary theme, with the resurgence of nationalism that emerged in the late sixties in Canada.

The dominant metaphor of the play is found in *Don Quixote* as portrayed by Franz Szabo's puppet theatre. A scene from Cervantes' famous satire, where the knight charges at the windmills, is staged by Szabo in the third act. Szabo, the artistic creator and 'soul' of the puppets, represents both the idealistic Don and the realistic Sancho Panza. Not easily discouraged, Szabo is tough as well as hopeful. His audience, the community representatives of education and recreation, are the mock giants who are really only windmills. As the journalist puts it, Szabo has met them and is safe. Cervantes' novel is commonly interpreted as a satire on the exaggerated chivalric romances of his time, but it can also be seen as an ironic story of an idealist frustrated in a materialistic world. By identifying the artist with both the knight and his squire, Davies stresses the artist's strength and persistence as well as his powers of vision. The foolish ''authorities'' on recreation and education embody cultural malnutrition in its most amusing form. They are finally routed in a wonderfully comic *débâcle*.

The play is set in Chilly Jim's ''equivocal establishment,'' built as a hangar and now a speak-easy or bootleg joint. In the background is the picturesque skyline of Kingston, with two cathedrals, a domed City Hall, towers of limestone churches and the river shipping in the harbour. Kingston artist Grant Macdonald created the original setting for the play.[3] The illicit liquor is fished up in a bucket from the river as required.

The plot is relatively simple. Nicholas Hayward is a youngish and talented professor who is determined to better himself by accepting an offer from an American university. His reasons are mixed, but chief among them is the need for more money in order to win Vanessa Medway. There is no promise in Canada, as yet, for men like him: only blank incomprehension. Canada is a nineteenth-century country, with the attitude of the pioneer towards scholarship and the arts. Idris Rowlands, a somewhat embittered senior professor, objects that Nicholas is too good to leave Canada for money, or to waste himself on shoddy scholarship, a reference to the book that Nicholas intends to churn out to ensure his American job.

Into this argument Davies introduces Franz Szabo, puppeteer from Prague, with his hundred-year-old hand-puppet Mr. Punch, his pictures of his lost marionettes, and his determination to create them anew. Szabo, a recent immigrant, is in danger of being deported because he lied about his age. Newspaperman Edward Weir vividly remembers seeing the puppet show in Prague in the thirties. The newspaperman offers to intercede with immigration officials on Szabo's behalf. The new Canadian becomes the catalyst for change in the other characters. Chilly, Weir, Vanessa and Nicholas are soon fired with enthusiasm and determined to help Szabo establish a puppet theatre in Canada. When Nicholas offers to write a play for the puppets, Vanessa reminds him of his scholarly book. Rowlands, who thinks that Vanessa is not the woman for Nicholas, suggests that he write a version of Apuleius' *The Golden Asse*. He says it is about a man who is turned into a jackass by a woman who does not understand the nature of her own enchantments. Vanessa and Nicholas look at one another awkwardly, sensing the parallel. It is a characteristic trick with Davies, in both fiction and drama, to use another work in this way as a comic or ironic analogue.

Act Two, one week later, features Szabo's confrontation with Ursula Simonds, Mattie Philpott, and Orville Tapscott. Ursula is a wealthy fellow-traveller; Mattie, Convenor of the Hobby Lobby and chairwoman of the local Recreation Commission; and Orville, a power in the field of education. All three have very much the same mentality. They view art as a tool, an aid to teaching political and social behaviour. This farcical trio illustrate Davies' hyperbolic but extremely comic portrait of the level of culture in contemporary Canada. By pitting them against Szabo, an unpretentious man whose artistic stature is established by the admiration of Chilly Jim and the intellectuals, Davies debunks their ideas while illustrating his own view of theatre and of art. Act Two also features a dramatic although not unreasonable change in Professor Rowlands. As long as Nicholas was set on going to the States, Rowlands, in the interest of conflict, was presented as a strong figure urging him to stay in Canada. As Nicholas' determination to stay grows slowly throughout the latter two thirds of the play, Rowlands' bitterness and disillusion is allowed to flower. He says he has had three good students in twenty-five years, and they are now all in the States: "This raw frost-bitten country has worn me out, and its raw frost-bitten people have numbed my heart." He says Nicholas is giving false encouragement to Szabo, who will never succeed in Canada with his puppets. They require a wiser, warmer audience than any he will find here. Why is Nicholas telling Szabo of Canadian opportunities while preparing to "turn traitor" himself? Nicholas accuses Rowlands of being obsessed by the idea of failure, and jealous because he has never been invited to go to the States or to return to England.

Ursula Simonds' talk of art as propaganda serves as a prelude to the entrance of the Moral Element, Mattie Philpott and Orville Tapscott. Mattie is loaded down with tortured metal and outraged leather, specimens of her own handicraft. Chilly Jim pretends to doubt her respectability ("So much jewellery. Kind of arouses suspicions") and advises her to keep her voice down and go home with the fellow she came with. Chilly Jim, a self-educated philosopher and an obviously happy man, tells the recreation director that some people consider *his* establishment the centre of the recreation field. Mattie and Orville are too busy with recreational activities to have any time for relaxation or enjoyment. Tapscott enjoys Chilly's fruit punch, which the audience suspects is spiked with gin, and says that such a tangy juice would go well in recreational juice bars in the city. Mattie and Orville view puppetry as a tot-to-teen activity calculated to encourage manual dexterity, a handicraft especially suited to the sub-teen girl. It is taught by a young woman who has taken a six-week College of Education summer course in it. Long skirts obviate the need for legs on the puppets and heads are from the five-and-ten. Mattie believes that there is no use expecting children to do anything difficult and Orville remarks on the value of audio-visuals, which reduce pupil resistance by cutting down pupil effort to the barest minimum. The purpose of education, in their minds, is to foster socially acceptable behaviour.

Szabo calls their ideas cheap and nasty, and refutes them in an impassioned speech: "Are fifteen generations of puppet masters to end with a harlot of a dirty dog who uses his art to tell nonsense? . . . If your nonsense is what your country believes, it is time your country got some sense." He says that the puppet master imparts something of his own soul to the puppets, making them more truly alive during the performance than himself. Tapscott, unmoved, trusts that Szabo will soon learn that in Canada art is proud to consider itself the handmaid of education. Szabo replies that he shall always believe that education is something which helps men to appreciate art. Irritated by Ursula's party line, Nicholas voices a theme found also in the short play *At the Gates of the Righteous*, namely, that external revolution does not effect real change: "the only revolutions that make any real difference to the world are revolutions in the hearts of individual men."

Act Two ends with a plan to stage a puppet play for Tapscott, who might get Szabo some work in connection with the public library system. Weir points out that Tapscott, "in his horrible way," is a man of some power. This prepares us for the windmill scene from *Don Quixote* in the next act.

Act Three presents the puppet show and the resolution of Nicholas' affairs. The play-within-a-play technique is a favorite with Davies. His playlet reveals the folly of the philistines in the most amusing way. They reduce art to morality, and morality to sentimental bathos. The puppet show is played against Weir's comic stage fright (he is managing the marionette of Sancho Panza), grotesque comments from Mattie and Orville, and Rowlands' drunken heckling of the self-righteous pair.

Before the puppet show, Vanessa and Nick have a serious discussion which leads to Vanessa's rejection of Nick. She quotes Sir Philip Sidney, "Tragedy concerneth a high fellow." Nick is a "high fellow," and his ruin would be a tragedy. If she accepted his love without loving in return, it would be the death of everything that is best in him. Nicholas has no time to reply before Mattie and Orville arrive to see the show.

Szabo announces that they are going to see a fragment from *Don Quixote*, the scene in which the knight charges against the windmills. Tapscott, who has been disappointed by the lack of bunnies and the Disney touch, is scandalized by the word *mistress*. He is not reassured by Szabo's aside that a knight and a member of the board of the 'Y' use the word in different senses. Mattie's objections centre on Sancho's realistic language. When he speaks of Rosinante as a bone-bag and his wife as an old scrubwoman, Mattie thinks it will foster class feeling and cruelty to dumb animals: "After all, if we can't have a play without making fun of others, it's a poor lookout, isn't it?" As for the knight himself, he won't do at all. Mattie disapproves of plays for children with maladjusted persons as the chief characters. Tapscott agrees: "You teach kids to make fun of a lunatic and first thing you know they'll all be delinquents." The recreational and educational experts condemn the play as an offence against thirty years of child psychology. Ursula condemns it for lacking a class message. She urges Szabo to make Sancho the proletariat, Don Quixote class government, and the windmills capitalism and private profit. All three view art as propaganda.

Rowlands explodes in fury, striking the puppet theatre with his stick and lashing out with his tongue. The old professor drives Mattie and Tapscott to the door in a rain of insults, like Christ driving the money changers from the temple. The educationists are donkeys in the temple of art; Rowlands curses them furiously: "Anathema! Anathema! Anathema!" Rowlands says he has judged and found them wanting, and that he destroyed the temple rather than see it profaned. He fears that theirs is the way in which Canada will react to the puppets.

Szabo praises Rowlands' honest rage but refuses to accept his conclusion. The educated and the uneducated like his work. As for the half-educated, it may require an act of God to lighten their darkness. Artists must be both tough and hopeful.

Nicholas now accepts Vanessa's rejection and says he has decided to stay in Canada. If Szabo can do it, so can he. Szabo thinks they will find, eventually, that the giants are only windmills.[4] The play closes with Rowlands' song, "Fortune, my foe,/Why dost thou frown on me?" The lyrics move from a description of temporary difficulties to an expression of hope: "Yet shall you smile again;/Nor shall my days/Pass all in grieving pain."

Buckety Murphy, an elderly drunken bum, is on stage for most of the play. Mavor Moore describes Buckety as a kind of disgraceful Greek chorus to the loftier business of the play: "Buckety Murphy has Art and Sensuality all hilariously mixed up; but could it be the old bum is onto something?"[5] Sensuality has more to do with art than has Mattie's moralizing. Buckety patronizes Szabo as he sits working at a puppet. The clichés about capitalism ("Weeds out the unfit. . . . The pace is killing. But the rewards are great") are extremely comic in the mouth of a man who has been weeded out from society, whose pace is leisurely and whose rewards are *nil*. He links himself with Szabo as a man who was once an artist. Buckety used to pose for photographs. His masterpiece, a series called "The Toilet of Hercules," was confiscated by the police. That ended Buckety's ventures in the realm of art.

Ursula Simonds, in contrast, is relatively ineffectual. With the exception of her suggested version for a proletarian Don Quixote, her sermons are flat and uninteresting, unlike the inspired grotesques, Mattie and Tapscott.

The effect of the puppet theatre is described by Weir as one of intensified reality. The puppets give "the whole delight and mystery of the theatre in miniature," in Rowlands' phrase. The puppet show induces a religious feeling in Nicholas and Chilly Jim. It supplies colour, warmth, gaiety, qualities once found in churches. To Mattie and Tapscott, the little theatre is simply a piece of handicraft. To the others, it evokes a mystery which answers to a human need. The combination of puppets and artist, infidels and judge in the Temple of Art is very good theatre indeed.

Hope Deferred, a short play published the year before *Fortune, My Foe*, lacks the latter's optimism. The full quotation from which the title is taken, "hope deferred maketh the heart sick," suggests the mood. In his Introduction to the play, which was part of Davies' first collection, *Eros at Breakfast*, Tyrone Guthrie writes of the difficulties of the one-act play and its necessity for a distinctive atmosphere — what Monica Gall's Irish drama teacher, in *A Mixture of Frailties*, called the "muhd." The mood of *Hope Deferred* is one of bitter gaiety, the ironic laughter of a sophisticate who sees that he is trapped.

The play is set in the city of Quebec in 1693, in the private apartment of the Governor of New France. Count Frontenac receives Bishop Laval and his aide and learns that the two bishops fiercely object to his plan to stage a production of Molière's *Tartuffe*. The enemies of art in this instance are not a ridiculous and sentimental bourgeoisie but a narrow and Jansenist priesthood who want the new land to be "good and great," especially good. Chimène, a Huron girl who has been educated in Paris, asks: "Are we to found a land without art here?" Laval says that he sees no reason why the people cannot be simple and good without play-acting, picture-making and tinkling music. Frontenac says the very climate of Canada imposes piety on her inhabitants. Chimène's reply, the key speech, is more serious: "It is because goodness without the arts demands a simplicity bordering on the idiotic. A simple man without the arts is a clod, or a saint, or a bigot: saints are very rare: clods and bigots are many. Are you trying to put my country into their hands?" While the setting is three hundred years old, the question is obviously of contemporary relevance.

The beautiful young Chimène is a symbolic rather than a realistic figure. Five years earlier, Frontenac had sent the Indian orphan to the Ursuline sisters to be educated as an actress. She had had instruction from one of the greatest actors of the Comédie Française, since the Count yearns to hear some good French declamation in the New World. Chimène's education in Paris (like that of the director of the play in *Tempest-Tost* or of Monica Gall in *A Mixture of Frailties*, and true to Davies' own experience in Oxford) symbolizes her acquisition of European culture which the Canadian artist must assimilate as his own cultural roots. The play opens with Chimène dancing for the Count what is described as a French dancing-master's notion of a Indian war dance. The exotic nature of her costume suggests the strangeness of a sophisticated art form such as Molière's drama in seventeenth-century Quebec. Her dissertation on the philosophy and art of kissing is the more comic for having been taught her, she says, by the good Ursuline Sisters.

The two bishops contrast with one another as well as with Chimène and the Count. The elderly Laval is calm and noble, while his coadjutor is fiery and fanatical. Both are dogmatic, but only Saint-Vallier is self-righteous. Frontenac explains to the bishops that one has to work to keep the wilderness at bay and to put salt in Quebec's porridge. He has already staged two plays in his chateau. He expects Chimène to provide the true accent and pace of Corneille, Racine and Molière.

Saint-Vallier reminds Frontenac that the Abbé Glandelet has recently preached a sermon in the cathedral proving to his own satisfaction that the play-goer incurs mortal sin. Saint-Vallier, who prides himself on being a man of the world, considers the Abbé to be lacking in subtlety. He pronounces that attendance at an innocent play is merely a venial sin, while attendance at an evil play is a mortal sin. The bishop is a true friend of the drama, Frontenac remarks with heavy irony.

The bishops consider Molière's *Tartuffe* to be a monstrous blasphemy. It presents piety, they say, in an unfavorable light. They have no confidence that simple souls, and especially the Indians, will be able to distinguish between false and true piety. Frontenac is indignant at the notion of keeping the intellectual tone of the entire country at the level suited to the simplest, but Saint-Vallier pleads for piety. The laxity of the English Sunday, he says, is already drawing Indians away from the French. The English can only be opposed by more missionaries, more strictness, and more piety.

Up until this point, Frontenac has defied the clergy. But if trade is threatened, he knows he will be called to account by the King. Chimène adds her plea, although the cause is obviously lost. Must art come last, she asks, and ''can real goodness and greatness come without it?'' Saint-Vallier rejects what Chimène calls art as frivolity, licence, and dangerous enquiry. Laval is more soothing: the things she loves may come, *after a time*. The religious philistines depart, and the Count assesses his trap: ''Trade makes its demands and morality backs it up — and where am I? These good men exert a dreadful pressure, Chimène . . . . There is no tyranny like that of organized virtue . . . . If trade and piety thrive, art can go to the devil: what a corrupt philosophy, what stupidity for a new country!''

The rejected artist decides to return to Paris where she can act. Her own land does not want her. Chimène is forced into the course of action rejected by Nicholas and Szabo in *Fortune, My Foe*. She beats her Indian drum, declaiming ''Espérance!'' Frontenac breaks off from their dance to hurl Saint-Vallier's moneybag to the floor, and the curtains close on Chimène's weeping. This round goes to the windmills.

Overlaid (1949) deals with many of the same themes as *Hope Deferred*. But the tone is lighter, the bitterness minimal, thanks to the outrageous and delightful vitality of Pop, the central character and the one-man "bohemian set of Smith township." In the Epilogue to the 1966 edition, Davies writes that the play is about the intellectual climate in our country and, specifically, about intellectual deprivation. Pop's need for what Davies calls the larger world of imagination, romance, and transporting emotion, has been denied him by the society in which he lives. He reaches out to this larger world in the only form it is available to him: the Saturday afternoon radio broadcasts of opera from New York. The play has been performed very frequently, something which suggests to Davies that Canadians are sufficiently aware of their cultural malnutrition to be ready to laugh at it.

The humour is blatantly hyperbolic. The fact that the three characters—Pop, a farmer of seventy, his forty-year-old daughter, and an insurance agent—are all caricatures does not prevent their being dramatically effective. Pop loves life; Ethel loves death, and Bailey, the agent, represents the community attitudes which reinforce Ethel and disapprove of Pop. The community is one where the existence of art is not even guessed at, as Sir Benedict Domdaniel puts it in *A Mixture of Frailties*. The play is set in a farm kitchen in rural Canada, but the attitudes represented could as readily be found in towns and cities. The action centres on the problem of what to do with an unexpected windfall of twelve hundred dollars from an insurance policy. The narrative device is an old one, but Davies' handling of it is fresh.

Ethel might be termed a spoiled artist, like Old Ma Gall, or a spoiled human being, having not only suppressed but successfully murdered her vital instincts. Frontenac, in *Hope Deferred*, spoke of the tyranny of organized virtue, and Chimène described the simple man without the arts as saint, clod or bigot. Ethel is no saint. She describes the opera broadcasts as "that row", and considers *emotion* a dirty word from which her fourteen-year-old son should be shielded. Ethel reveals herself in her scorn for the things Pop values and, even more clearly, in her yearning for a granite headstone. The dream of her heart is to have an impressive family cemetery plot on the crest of the hill, complete with chain fence and a great big block of grey granite: dignified, quiet, and the finest in the cemetery. Her idea of family togetherness is togetherness in death. Earlier, she has described the earthly reward for work and duty as the reputation for never asking anything of anybody. The ultimate goal in such ironic self-sufficiency is, very logically, death. Much of the play's humour depends upon contrasts and incongruities. Pop sits in a decrepit old top hat and white workman's gloves (he informs Ethel that white gloves are "*dee rigger*" for opera) making comments like "Attaboy! Yippee!" and "Hot dog!" in response to the announcer's well-bred voice coming over the radio. Most comic is the female radio voice which erupts intermittently with remarks like "If our lives lack beauty, we are poor indeed . . . " and "render life gracious with the boon of art." The remarks are true but grotesquely foreign to the kitchen scene, farcically incongruous. So is our mental vision of Pop together with the New York socialite who is president of the Opera Radio Guild. Pop is a paid-up member of the Guild and threatens to call up the president ("she's my kind") when he goes to New York. The two radio voices bring another world on stage, one which points up the narrowness of Smith Township.

The news that he has twelve hundred dollars coming to him sets Pop happily dreaming of a New York trip, a Grand Binge of wine, women and song. *Song* includes the Metropolitan Opera House which is gloriously mixed in Pop's mind with a burlesque theatre. He tells the scandalized Ethel and George Bailey that God likes music and naked women, and he's happy to follow His example. The agent refuses to give him the money for such a spree, but Pop shrewdly calls his bluff. Pop's dialogue with Ethel brings out the joylessness of her life and the local reverence for work, self-denial and duty. Pop has had enough of these. Somebody, he says, has got to start ignoring the so-called necessities if they are ever to have any of the things that really make life worth living — the mysterious but enriching things that he is trying to suggest through his New York dream.

Pop's dead wife is invoked several times; her fate suggests Ethel's. Mother and daughter are two of a kind. Pop describes his wife as always having worked, if not at home then over at the church. At forty-five or fifty she broke down and was taken to a mental institution. Emotional undernourishment is Pop's diagnosis. He predicts that Ethel is going the same way. Ethel agrees that she is following in her mother's trail, but sees nothing ironic in this. She does think, however, that two such hard-working women deserve the best in headstones.

Moved by pity, and temporarily overlaid, as he puts it, by Ethel's belief in her own goodness (cf. "the tyranny of organized virtue," Frontenac's phrase), Pop endorses his insurance cheque over to Ethel. The curtain line is Pop's, as he assures Ethel that his depression is only temporary "an' that stone'll rest lighter on me that it will on you." Ethel's coveted gravestone is a symbol for the dead hand of the cultural attitudes she embodies, a debased form of puritanism such as the type Hugh MacLennan attacks in *The Precipice* and *Each Man's Son*.

In the Preface to the 1968 reprint of *The Voice of the People* (*Four Favorite Plays*), Davies writes that the play is intended only to amuse but has its roots in truth. There are plenty of people like the Mortons, and a few like Sam North. During the twenty years Davies was a newspaper editor, he received many letters to the editor which were on the level of Shorty's outburst. The play is a light and amusing farce. We might call it a "throw-away," the term Irving Layton applies to some of his minor poems. A single comic incident drives towards a concluding moral epigram, in the manner of Aesop's fables: "He that answereth a matter before he heareth it, it is folly and shame unto him.''

The scene is the kitchen of a small town barber. Shorty Morton's ignorance is exceeded only by his self-confidence and his refusal to be confused by the facts. When a friend phones to say that there is a letter to the editor complaining about the increase in barber-shop prices, Shorty sets to work to write an indignant reply. His temper is already frayed by the delay in his dinner. The Morton's stove is being repaired by electrician, Sam North.

Sam is an engaging character, type of the rural philosopher. His common sense and dry wit make him an excellent foil to Shorty. Sam has read the Bible through three times. His biblical knowledge is a frequent source of humour. Shorty's tendency to ascribe various clichés or folk sayings to the Bible provokes Sam's laconic ''Nope.'' Shorty's appeal to the electrician to hurry with his job (''Sam! Sam!'') is met with ''speak, Lord, for thy servant heareth.''[6] Sam, as his name suggests, is the prophet of a northern land.

Through the Morton's self-indulgent teen-ager, sixteen-year-old Myrtle, Davies ''gets off a few good ones'' at the expense of contemporary methods in art and education. Art class consists of an exercise in collage. As Myrtle puts it, ''we have to bring some junk and arrange it interestingly in the box.'' The prize for the best box is a book by ''Salvador Daley'' — an Irishman, Myrtle suspects. Mrs. Morton's idea of a first-class education is a collection of facts such as the ones that fill up small gaps in the newspaper. Myrtle is unable to help her father compose his letter, since she had learned only The Friendly Letter, the Congratulation or Condolence, and Applying for a Position. She studies Latin but can't help to translate ''Pro Bono Publico,'' the signature of the letter which has so annoyed Shorty. However, her Latin teacher has warned her not to translate Latin words by the English words they resemble, so Myrtle assures Shorty that ''if 'publico' looks like public you can bet that's one thing it doesn't mean!''

Shorty has jumped to the conclusion that the Letter to the Editor, which he does not read until he has finished composing his own, was written by Townsend, an old enemy who hates to pay for a shave. Shorty's letter libels Townsend and leads into a humorous anecdote which illustrates the latter's stinginess. Having finished his repairs to the stove, Sam offers to deliver Shorty's letter: to himself. Sam is Pro Bono Publico. The play ends with the biblical epigram.

At My Heart's Core (1950) is a curious play with certain inner tensions and inconsistencies which have not been fully resolved. It is a play about temptation and deep inner longings. It is also about duty and self-sacrifice. In *Fortune, My Foe* Nicholas' tempter, Vanessa Medwell, is external to him. In *At My Heart's Core* the apparent tempter, neighbour Cantwell, is a personification of the desires of the three women whom he tempts. Professor Rowlands describes Vanessa as a temptress who does not understand herself or Nicholas. The sophisticated Cantwell understands his victims only too well.

Davies' closing words in his interview with Donald Cameron are about the responsibility and self-knowledge which an artist must bear. Being an artist, he said, implies "a duty to be true to your abilities in so far as you can and as deeply as you can."[7] Two of the three central female characters in *At My Heart's Core*, Susanna Moodie and Catherine Parr Traill, are unwilling to be true to their particular genius, to the best art and scholarship that lie in their power to accomplish. Cantwell understands their natures. He understands their longing for self-fulfilment in these areas and reveals it to them, *knowing they will do nothing about it*. "I pitied the women very deeply," Davies remarked, adding that *At My Heart's Core* is a Women's Lib play.[8]

Davies' Preface to the original edition speaks of the play as dealing with a problem which is widespread and continuing. He has chosen to place it in Canada in 1837, which makes the characters early Victorians wrestling with all the hardships of pioneer farms. The play is not intended as a naturalistic reproduction of contemporary life, and the playwright suggests that its successful performance requires "a judicious dash of exaggeration."

We are thus alerted to the contemporary nature of one of Davies' major themes. The philistines are ever with us: in Frontenac's Quebec, in Moodie's Upper Canada, and in Davies' native Ontario. Cantwell, the demonic tempter, and Phelim, the drunken Irish bard around whom the sub-plot revolves, are the only two characters in *At My Heart's Core* who really believe in art. Phelim is a self-styled poet and story-teller. Back in Ireland, his stories were needed and loved. In Upper Canada, the busy pioneers have "the maggot o' respectability in their brains." He tells Susanna Moodie that they two are the songbirds that aren't wanted in this bitter land of industry and politics. Cantwell, critic and connoisseur, praises art in more formal terms (art gives form and meaning to life, he tells Mrs. Moodie) and lays bare the materialistic quality of Canadian ambitions. There is a period, Cantwell says, between poverty and affluence during which men feel no need for poetry and stories: "And there is a sort of education which forgets that the mind needs not only to be polished, but oiled." The middle of the twentieth century finds us still in that interregnum. Still short of oil.

The play is set in the backwoods homestead of Frances and Thomas Stewart, Member of the Legislative Council for Douro, Upper Canada. The setting is the house, which is open to the audience like a doll's house, plus the forest approach. This ingenious arrangement is well suited to the action. We are prepared for the three temptations which occupy the second act by the women's naïve assumption, stated at the end of Act One, that lack of temptation is one of the few advantages which the backwoods have to offer. Their husbands are all away at York defending the government against Mackenzie's rebels.

Mrs. Stewart's temptation comes first but I shall treat it last. Cantwell flatters Mrs. Traill by telling her of the high opinion of her work held by a famous natural scientist. Mrs. Traill knows of Mr. Sheppard, whom Cantwell has met, and has been forced to refuse his offer of collaboration in the preparation of a book on Canadian flora because her work as a settler's wife does not leave her sufficient time. Cantwell urges the claims of genius: if she has it in her to do notable scientific work, why should she put this second to pioneer drudgery? Mrs. Traill retorts that new countries require sacrifice, as do one's husband and children. Cantwell insists that there is no reason why her work should play second fiddle. She leaves him, visibly upset.

The tempter uses Byron as the bait for Susanna Moodie. Byron, Cantwell says, was glad of the latter's opinion on his verse. The Irish novelist Maria Edgeworth is another of Cantwell's acquaintances. He holds out to Moodie the prospect of writing as well as Edgeworth if she would put her work first instead of subordinating it, as Mrs. Traill does, to husband and country.

The height of each temptation, the point when the shaft finds the heart's core, is marked by the sound of a hunting horn: an effective device. After three such soundings, Mr. Stewart returns home, puzzled that no one has noticed his horn and come to meet him, and even more puzzled by the confused and dejected state of the three women. The third act consists of Stewart's informal "trial" of the man who has so upset the three women.

Davies has said that he intended to show the terrible sacrifice of abilities required by pioneering conditions and intended to *mock* the concept of the noble pioneer intent on forging a great land. The central irony is that the temptations offered to Traill and Moodie are the truth: "They were living false lives, lying lives. They have more refinement than sense." Cantwell is a genuine aristocrat, Davies added, and his ideas will inevitably seem demonic to bourgeois minds. Cantwell's "Byronic-Satanic" manners and appearance play upon the popular misconception of Byron, and Mrs. Moodie is more impressed by the fact that Byron is an aristocrat than by the fact that he is a poet.

There are several problems which come between these intentions and the resulting play. The first is Cantwell's name. If Cantwell is the devil speaking truth, surely a less pejorative name would lessen the confusion. In Act Three of the slightly revised second edition of the play,[9] Davies has deleted a *canting* remark about the poor from Cantwell's part. The result of this deletion is to make Cantwell more sympathetic and sensible at this point. A small matter, but indicative. With such a name, and with the emphasis upon his devilish aspects, the audience is unprepared to accept his advice. The psychological explanation as to why Cantwell has purposely upset the women (they slighted his wife) may be romantic but tends to make us dismiss the validity of his arguments.

Another problem lies in the fact that Davies has made the women's defence of their sacrifice too effective. When Mrs. Traill says that a new country brings hope and demands sacrifice, it seems to ring true. When she says that her life is not pitiful but full of interest, we believe her. Susanna Moodie is a more comic figure, with a hint of the drill-sergeant in her manner and a comic obsession with Methodists. But both Mrs. Traill and Mrs. Stewart evoke our sympathy and admiration.

Mrs. Stewart is the real heroine of the play and the only character with a sense of humour. It is slightly confusing that her temptation is meant to be resisted whereas for the other two women, resistance means self-betrayal. In a hunting incident in Ireland, Cantwell had discovered that Lord Rossmore wears Mrs. Stewart's picture in a locket around his neck. He tempts her to betray her husband with thoughts of Lord Rossmore and his brilliant world of fashion which she has exchanged for the backwoods. Such beauty and charm, Cantwell urges, are wasted here. In a romantic finale by the fireside with her husband, Mrs. Stewart tells him what has happened, and assures him that Cantwell arouses not regret but only discontentment disguised as regret. Her marriage is a happy one, and Cantwell's temptation is powerless against it. The married couple come across as being very much in love, a situation which is likely to confuse a modern director. One questions the term ''Women's Lib,'' since the heroine and the only woman proof against the temptation of regret, is the one whose destiny lies within a traditional sexist role.

The play has an amusing sub-plot which revolves around Phelim Brady, his foster-daughter Honour who is soon to be his bride, their new-born child, and the corpse of his first wife which he has placed on the roof as a precaution against wolves. Various scuffles, physical and verbal, between Phelim, Honour, and Mrs. Stewart's Indian servant Sally provide comic relief. Mrs. Traill and Mrs. Moodie's dispute over the care and handling of babies' heads provides an amusing episode in the first act, and Stewart's imitation of the famous clown Grimaldi enlivens the third with a bawdy song and a jig.

The parallel technique, demonstrated here in having not one but several temptings, is an effective trick, one that Davies uses frequently. Fairy stories and tales of mythic adventures also use parallel incidents, and one is reminded of this sort of literature when Cantwell asks Mrs. Moodie, ''who ever heard a sister praised without wishing to try her own luck?'' The Victorian atmosphere is well sustained and allows for satirical jibes such as ''not before the servants'' and ''As we are all females it is not necessary for Susanna to conceal the fact she has an appetite.'' In brief, *At My Heart's Core* is a romantic comedy of great charm, marred by ambiguity as to its central intent. Cantwell's arguments do not have the force of Nicholas Hayward's last speech in *Fortune, My Foe*: ''let Canada do what she will with us, we must stay.''

Notes to Chapter Three

1. See Robertson Davies, *A Mixture of Frailties*, Laurentian Library 7 (Toronto: Macmillan, 1968), pp.55, 303.

2. Mavor Moore, *Four Canadian Playwrights* (Toronto:Holt, Rinehart and Winston of Canada, 1973), p.12.

3. A picture of the original setting is found in Moore, *Four Canadian Playwrights*, p.18.

4. M.W. Steinberg, ''Don Quixote and the Puppets,'' *Canadian Literature*, 7 (Winter, 1961), p.47, finds the ending somewhat pat and sentimental, yet defends Nicholas' decision as being ''in character.''

5. Moore, *Four Canadian Playwrights*, p.13.

6. See 1 Samuel 3:9, concerning God's call to Samuel.

7. Donald Cameron, *Conversations with Canadian Novelists*, pp.45-46.

8. Conversation, 20 August 1974. All opinions ascribed to Davies in connection with *At My Heart's Core* refer to this conversation, unless another source is given.

9. See Robertson Davies, *At My Heart's Core and Overlaid. Two Plays* (Toronto:Clarke, Irwin, 1966), p.77.

4

The Guise of Beauty

Throughout twenty-five years of writing plays, certain related themes continue to recur in Davies' work: freedom, honour, romantic love, love of life, love of beauty. His recent television drama, "Brothers in the Black Art," poses the question, "In what guise does a man invite beauty to touch his life?" In this chapter I propose to examine five plays with this query in mind: two from the late forties (*At the Gates of the Righteous* and *King Phoenix*); one from the fifties (*A Jig for the Gypsy*); and two unpublished ones from the seventies ("Leaven of Malice" and "Brothers in the Black Art").

At the Gates of the Righteous (1949) is Davies' most Shavian play. It employs Shaw's inversion technique and breathes his hatred of cant. The play develops one of Shaw's favorite themes, namely, the respect which society accords to the successful scoundrel.[1] Davies' preface to the paperback reprint (1968) says that the play has apparently puzzled spectators: "Audiences do not greatly care for inversions of popular opinions, and when they are combined with mockery of our hallowed, pioneer past the mixture may prove disturbing." Davies speaks of two themes in the play: the first, that roguery flourishes more readily within the law than outside it; the second, that revolution is not the path to freedom.[2] The discovery that the only real revolt is in the mind is a bitter pill to young Fingal McEachern.

The play develops a delightful cross-patterning of idealistic cant and common-sense debunking. Both sides are guilty of cant. Both sides have an artificial rhetoric in defence of their cherished illusions, while both are quick to spot artificiality in the opposing point of view. The thrust and counter-thrust in the play illustrates the tension which Davies sees as central to the comic spirit.

The year is 1860; the scene, a country house in Upper Canada. A woman is playing the harmonium, badly. The relationship between the four characters in the opening scene and their occupation (which turns out to be highway robbery) remains mysterious for a few minutes. A Byronic young man and a girl in boy's clothing jump through a window and offer to join the others. After some amusing confusion and a reception which is not at all what they bargained for, the romantic young Fingal informs the robbers that he and Jessie are in revolt against Society. Fingal seeks soul-fulfilment, glory, and Power in Action. He is against hypocrisy and superstition, and thinks of religion as a chain forged by priests to enslave mankind, a trick to keep the poor poor and the rich rich. Power is the only good, so he has "fled to the forest" to join Bad Bill Balmer's band. Bill, in Fingal's view, lives by Power alone and makes war upon the hypocrisy of Society. Fingal's romantic clichés are comically capitalized. The youth despises money and aspires to be a Free Soul.

The robbers proceed to shatter Fingal's expectations. The pair are half-stripped as a preliminary to being shot. Where is the traditional highwayman's chivalry? Ronnie, who has narrowly missed becoming an Anglican clergyman because of a scandal over mission funds, explains that they are professionals and do not allow chivalry to eat into their profits.

By this time, the counter-rhetoric of Bill's gang is in full play. We have been introduced to the thieves in a scene which parodies a Sunday afternoon in respectable society. Effie's knowledge of music and musical terms would hardly have satisfied the Traills or the Moodies. A newspaper review of *The Complete Phrenologist* moves Bill to voice the hope that they can settle down somewhere to teach music and read heads: "We'd be a genuine acquisition to any go-ahead place. Science and Art: just what the country needs." Effie is the soul of conventionality. She is upset by Jessie's use of the word *mistress*, and outraged by Fingal's reference to her running away with Bill. Bill's and Ronnie's comments make clear that Effie's married state is more equivocal than she cares to think, but Effie has a vision of respectability which is as comic as Fingal's vision of rebellion. Bill sums up Fingal's fine phrases as Atheism and Free Love. Effie is further scandalized by these terms, and indignant at being called a *woman*. She's no woman, she tells Fingal. She's a *lady*. A married lady! Fingal's unvarnished language in this connection contrasts comically with his Rousseauesque phrases about exulting with one's mate in the forest glades.

Bad Bill's interest in phrenology, introduced earlier, now leads to a most amusing scene, as the highwayman applies his favorite science to an assessment of Fingal's character. Phrenology, the deduction of mental faculties from the shape of the skull, was extraordinarily popular in nineteenth-century Canada.[3] Fingal proves to have large amativeness, small acquisitiveness, and no sublimity at all. Effie is sceptical, but Bill has shown to his own satisfaction the reason for Fingal's disapproval of religion and respectability. He is obviously unqualified for a partnership.

Motherhood is the next sacred cow to be debunked. Parents are part of the social order against which Fingal is revolting. The thieves are profoundly shocked. "Why, boy, worship of motherhood is as universal and as sacred as the worship of God," Bill declares. Effie and Ronnie give touching tributes to their mothers, but Bill achieves the heights (or depths) of comic bathos in his story of being led away from his dear mother after his first crime, while promising to "make it up to her." Davies' parody of Victorian sentiment reaches a climax in Bill's peroration: "Upper Canada is, and always will be, a land where motherhood is held in honour and where e'en the sacred name of Wife must give place of honour to that simplest but mightiest of words—Ma!" Ronnie declares that Bill's place is in politics. Bill returns the compliment. Ronnie will make a high-grade evangelist, a business far more profitable than highway robbery.

Bill assures Fingal that despite a few misunderstandings with banks and stagecoaches, they honour the law. Society is as sound as a bell, and the best pickings are always *inside* its rules: Davies' ironic theme. The fat of the jest is that the highway robbers exhibit a storekeeper's mentality. Fingal has helped them to realize that they are wasting their time outside the law. Old Angus, their wounded partner, has conveniently expired in his chair. Their share of his loot will help to set them up as phrenology professor and church organist.

Fingal and Jessie are tied to their chairs, and Old Angus is given a one-minute funeral. Fingal is disgusted by what he calls a "maudlin display of self-delusion, hypocrisy, cant and shoddy thinking." Ronnie says that both Bill and Fingal are romantics, whereas he is a realist who recognizes infinite shades of grey between the light and the dark. It is no surprise to Ronnie to see Bill change from the grey of gun-metal to the silver grey of the statesman's frock coat. If Fingal, son of the Presbyterian minister, ever preaches a sermon on the day's events, Ronnie recommends Proverbs 14:9 as the text: "The evil bow before the good, and the wicked at the gates of the righteous." Effie's parting advice to Jessie is to find a man with some principles, "like Bill," and to do nothing till she has her ring. The thieves can be heard galloping away, and the trussed pair are left to reflect on the unsatisfactory plight of the revolutionary.

Ronnie's affected English accent is annoying in print (he is described as having an English upper class accent, and his *r* is printed as *w* throughout) but might be effective on stage. Old Angus is a farcical character who does nothing but snore periodically and terrify the youngsters with some fancy shooting.

The strength of the play lies in Bill's and Fingal's equal but opposite rhetorics of respectability and revolution. Had Davies parodied only one of these positions and defended the other, his audiences might have been less puzzled, but the play would have been much the poorer. The alternatives offered are not nonsense and sense but two types of nonsense. One debunks the other, and both combine to create a burlesque of social attitudes which exposes hypocrisy and pretence. The secondary theme, that the revolutions that matter are interior ones, is echoed by Nicholas in *Fortune, My Foe*. Freedom wears a comic mask in *At the Gates of the Righteous*.

King Phoenix, set in a mythic England, is an allegory of Eden and of the restlessness in the heart of man which drives him out of that happy state. Cole, the old but merry king, is the essence of laughter, joy, vitality. He is opposed by his chief minister, Archdruid Cadno, whose name is Welsh for *fox*. In "The Centennial Play," a character named Fox is described as representing the part of the country which is for material things and greed. Cadno is as crafty, clever, energetic and shrewd as that other Fox. He symbolizes not simply greed but change, and the type of mind which welcomes change and foolishly equates it with progress. The man who can direct change is the great man of his time, as the giant Gogmagog tells King Cole.

The romantic and melodramatic plot includes two attempted murders by the Archdruid and the magical appearance of a giant's ghost. Act Two develops the theme, while the first and third acts carry the major action. Act Three is a magnificent spectacle where Cole, who dies laughing, is identified with the sun as the very spirit of life. His daughter Helena dons his ceremonial paint and takes her father's place, announcing that before sunset she shall be wedded to Prince Leolin, but until noon she is wedded only to the will of her father.

The allegory can be interpreted even more specifically. Cadno, who is supervising the building of a vast new temple being constructed to embody the principles of Druidical science, represents modern technology, and Cole's land, a pastoral one poised on the brink of change, suggests Canada in the process of becoming an industrial and technological culture.

Cadno believes that what is "unnatural" must be destroyed. It is ironic that he finds Cole's laughter and vitality unnatural. Cadno hates Cole as a stumbling block in the path of progress. In grandiose and pseudo-religious language, Cadno tells the merchant Idomeneus that Druidical science represents a change from the domination of Nature to the domination of artifice. By *artifice* he does not mean *art*, which is already highly developed in Cole's kingdom. Under Cole, Nature flourishes unchecked. Cadno intends to train and cultivate Nature, to subject her to his will. His Druidical science will be sold to the people as religion rather than as science, since religion is better suited, Cadno believes, to a mean understanding, and credulous people can be more easily managed. In a quiet interval at the end of the second act, Idomeneus and a shepherd sum up the differences between Cadno and the king, and the larger meaning of their conflict. Cadno's hope "to get at the very sources of life itself" is threatened by Cole's "mirthful largeness," which makes change appear needless. Cadno is a man of action; Cole, a man of repose.

Cole first tastes his own mortality in the grove of sacred oak trees after talking with the ghost of the giant Gogmagog. Davies' handling of parallelism and inversion can be seen here. The giant was once as evil as Cole is benevolent. Both are confronted with Cadno, spirit of change. Gogmagog is a shambling shell of his former self, a comi-pathetic figure. He wistfully recalls his prime, when he had only to roar and men scampered like ants from an ant hill. He had attempted to trick Cadno by sending him off on an impossible quest (a tale straight out of classic fairy lore), but Cadno had tricked the giant and had slain him by physical, not magical means. The whispering leaves of the sacred oaks tell Cole that his life is a dream. Death is a paradoxical awakening to the changes going on around him. Cole later tells Idomeneus that the poison he was given in the woods has succeeded, where Cadno's poison failed. Gogmagog was once considered to be invincible. Talking with him, Cole realizes that all things perish: "When a man knows with all his body and all his soul that he is mortal, he is already dead."

Prince Leolin, Helena's suitor, is a high-minded young man with a sentimentalized code of honour and duty. Through Helena, who has a fair measure of her father's spirit, Davies mocks the foolish form of nobility embodied in the prince. "You pompous self-honouring toad!" she tells Leolin. "You are so stuffed with honour and high aspirations that you are unbearable." The prince has refused to cooperate with Cadno in his plot to poison Cole. Cadno then decrees that Leolin is the human sacrifice demanded by the gods for the feast of the vernal equinox. Leolin makes no objection: the gods require a sacrifice, and his faith sustains him. As he waits for sunrise and for the moment of sacrifice, Helena cuts through his generalized benevolence with taunts and kisses, biting his lip till the blood flows, awakening him to real passion, and greater self-knowledge.

Leolin's death is prevented by King Cole, who offers himself by falling from the high altar at the sacrificial moment. His fall takes place off-stage but is reflected onstage by the awed faces of those who are watching him and by the beauty of their words, a much more dramatic technique than the literal presentation of Cole's death. The king has taken the crown of mistletoe, the victim's headdress intended for the prince. Shouts from the crowd, followed by sudden silence, alert the principals to Cole's actions. They see him dancing at the top of the Druids' stone circle, magnificent and awesome. His hair is green in the sunlight, like the crown of mistletoe. His face, painted ceremonially by his beloved brewer, Boon Brigit, burns like the Sun himself. He looks and dances like a god — and falls to the altar below as it is touched by the first light of spring.

The broken body of the King is carried onstage. Cole tells Helena he will live on in her, and her children, and her children's children. "My people will remember me forever as a merry man, whose death was his best joke." Laughing, he dies. The people take the King's death as the consecration sacrifice, and Cadno is balked of his intended victim, Leolin. Idomeneus says that Cole died laughing in order to show us the holiness and greatness of laughter such as his. Helena prepares to celebrate rather than mourn. Her father, and her own inheritance, is the spirit of life and joy which is constantly renewed like the phoenix of the play's title.

Davies' imagination was originally sparked by reading *The History of the Kings of Britain* by the twelfth-century chronicler Geoffrey of Monmouth. The play is a colourful spectacle, especially its third act, which is set in the interior

of a large tent used as the robing and property room of the Druidical cere-
monies. The tent walls are hung with ceremonial regalia. There are willow
baskets of sacred snakes, and a willow cage for the human sacrifice. For the first
part of the act, Prince Leolin occupies the sacrificial cage as he talks with
Helena. This heightens suspense by reminding us of how little time is left to the
lovers. Past the entrance to the tent moves a religious procession, with other
cages of sacrificial victims and flaming hoops and torches.

Davies observes the classical unity of time: twelve hours. The action moves
from sunset to sunrise through the night of the vernal equinox. The shepherd
Lug acts the part of a Greek chorus. He tells Boon Brigit that she is wasting her
time in making a painkiller for Prince Leolin, who will refuse to drink it. Lug
speaks of the belly and the heart, and the pain and joy appropriate to each. The
merchant, for example, lives on the level of the belly: belly comfort for a belly
man, Lug says. The prince knows "pain-joy," a fiercer joy which comes from
"pain-faith." Cole praises the laughter of the belly as being good in its way.
His own laughter, however, is from the heart. It is a glorious and divine
drunkenness. Lug speaks the line which holds the play's theme: "For the
laughing man the skies stand still; only the dark and glowering man can push
them on." Laughter, the divine gift to man, stands *outside* time; change, which
brings death and decay, attempts to destroy the Golden Age of joy. A drinking
song in honour of John Barleycorn, alias Bacchus, alias Nature's perpetual
renewal under the sun reminds the audience that the play is, among other
things, a modern version of a fertility ritual. Cadno has no part in John
Barleycorn: he does not drink. Lug describes Cadno as a man who is his own
poison and who will soon die of spleen. The king is imaged as a well at which
lesser people fill their buckets. His daughter's name reminds us of Helen of
Troy, the fabled beauty whose face launched a thousand ships. But laughter of
the heart is the true guise of beauty in *King Phoenix*.

A Jig for the Gypsy is a play about love and politics, a combination which the
playwright considers natural, even "inseparable." It offers two romances, one
expected, which falls through, and one unexpected, which ends with a gypsy
wedding over the broom. The setting, the general atmosphere, and the plot are
all highly romantic. As a counterbalance, however, Davies debunks ideas
which he considers to be sentimental rather than truly romantic. The play, in
short, is a fine example of Davies' usual unconventional combination of
romance and ironic wit. As one of the characters puts it in the play, "It never
does to underestimate the ironical strain in the Welsh character."

The play is set in 1885 in the beautiful border country of North Wales near the
market town of Caerhowell. Davies tells us in his Preface that this play had been
in his mind for some time. It was originally sparked by a reading of *Zadkiel's
Dream Book* during an Easter vacation in Wales in 1938. His father's family
had lived for generations in North Wales and Davies was attracted both by ties
of sentiment and by the charm of its history and its people. Romance and

politics go together because the ambitions of politicians are romantic, especially when they are reformers with idealistic notions about the perfectibility of mankind through political action: "To me, there is nothing in the least odd about linking politics and fortune-telling in a play; they have been too often linked in reality, even in Canada."[4]

It is election week. The play covers eight days, ending on election night. Caerhowell has been a Tory seat for seventy years, but now Sir John Jebson seems to have a good chance of winning the seat for Gladstone's reformers. Grocer Richard Roberts, Sir John's supporter, thinks that a Whig victory would be assured if Benoni Richards, a local gypsy woman well-known as a fortune teller, would read his tea cup and forecast success. Many people who would not admit to it believe in fortune telling. Alexander the Great, King Arthur and Caesar all had their soothsayers. Benoni will appeal to the voters' imagination, as Richards puts it, "which is as safe a card as you can play in Wales." The grocer sends his daughter Bronwen to ask Benoni to read Sir John's cup.

Bronwen, a beautiful and impressionable young woman, is secretly in love with Sir John's secretary Edward Vaughan. Vaughan thinks of politics as something which will set all men free, and make their lives beautiful. Bronwen mouths Vaughan's beliefs which are lifted from John Ruskin's *Sesame and Lilies* and his just-published *Fors Clavigera:Letters to the Workmen and Labourers of Great Britain*. (Similarly, Carol, in *Hunting Stuart*, echoes the psychological clichés of her young man Fred.) Poacher Jack the Skinner reacts ironically to Bronwen's cant. She calls him an honest workman and a noble spectacle, yet is unwilling to associate with him. As for singing at his labour, Skinner suggests that if he did so he would not last an hour in the castle park, nor would her father survive a week in the grocery trade. The parody of Ruskin's social aesthetic is used to show up the self-importance and humourless quality of Edward Vaughan, whom Bronwen finally rejects.

Davies rarely misses an opportunity to satirize the pretentions of the middle class. Both Bronwen and Vaughan have something of the sentimental high-mindedness of Prince Leolin in *King Phoenix*. Bronwen considers modesty, Victorian style, to be a woman's chief jewel, and greatly admires Vaughan's earnest ambition. Benoni tells Bronwen that her idea of love is foolishness, and that she belongs to the class where everything that is important either seems coarse or is beyond her understanding. Why should she marry the first man who takes her fancy? Marriage and love don't come in the same package, Benoni says, and "there's more to marriage than four bare legs in a blanket."

Comic highlights in Act One include the scepticism of Sir John and Edward Vaughan towards the fortune-telling scheme, followed by their complete conversion after Benoni's favourable reading; the reading itself, with Sir John's and his secretary's inflated interpretations of every remark and the conclusions they jump to; Sir John's pretensions to Welsh intuition, on the strength of one distant relative; his miserliness towards Benoni, thinly disguised as principle;

his instructions to Roberts to remind him to give him his views on the mystical nature of Radicalism; and Jack the Skinner's deft spreading of the prophetic tea cup reading: ''Spread's too coarse a word for what I done! Not spread: I sprinkled it. I hinted; I winked; I smiled; I let 'em coax: then I told 'em not to breathe a word to a living soul. That was my masterstroke! In half an hour it was everywhere.''

The hint of terror which often accompanies Davies' (like Eisengrim's) effects of mystery and beauty is found here in the feeling, which builds from the end of Act One, that the election results will bring bad luck to Benoni, no matter who wins. Her gypsy blood gives warning, but too late. Benoni's name means ''child of sorrow.'' The first act closes on Benoni brooding beneath a darkening sky. She shudders, goes quickly in, and can be heard bolting the door.

Act Two, in mid-week, contains a comic succession of visitors who climb the hill to see Benoni because of the furor precipitated by her reading of Sir John's cup. Poor Benoni finds it unsafe to go abroad to sell her goats' milk. Mr. Pugh, a photographer of Radical political persuasion, is determined to martyr himself by putting a photo of Benoni with her teapot in the window of his establishment. His rhetoric is full of sentimental bathos. An Anglican clergyman comes to inform the gypsy of the archdeacon's displeasure and to urge her to recant. Benoni tells him that he and she are both magicians, two eggs from the same nest, although he may not like to think so. Vaughan comes to request a reading for himself and is told he's a spoiled preacher. There is a comic love scene where Vaughan spouts Ruskin to Bronwen and generally acts the proper Victorian suitor while the girl begins to suspect that perhaps Vaughan is *not* her fate. Three Tory supporters come from the Earl to threaten Benoni with the loss of her house and land unless she signs a retraction. The Earl's valet, known as the Backstairs Earl, apes his master's mannerisms. Fewtrell's vanity is comic, but Benoni's future looks dark and her fear is genuine. The act ends dramatically with the gypsy tearing open the front of her gown and cursing Fewtrell to become as bent in body as he is in soul.

The third act takes place on the evening of election day. Bronwen asks Benoni about her affair with Captain Lloyd, who died in the Crimean War. It was a love match, Benoni advises the girl, but would never have made a successful marriage. She advises Bronwen not to marry Vaughan. News comes of the election results. The Liberals are in, and Benoni is out. The Earl's man tells her she must leave by eight in the morning. Sir John is in no mood to help her since his ambition and political naïveté have cost him the cabinet post he coveted.

Conjuror Jones has been mentioned briefly in the first two acts as ''the great man of magic'' in the neighbourhood. The conservatives, meeting fire with fire, have tried to obtain his support for their candidate. The Conjuror now arrives on Benoni's doorstep, accompanied by thunder and lightning. The magician is a shrivelled but lively old man, an impressive figure. He tells

Benoni that her curse has taken its effect on the Earl's valet, who is now ill in bed. Fewtrell has tricked the Conjuror, cutting him out of the castle's candle trade upon which his livelihood depends. The Conjuror proposes marriage to Benoni, who at first refuses. He presses the economic benefits of the proposal: she is without shelter, he is without livelihood. If she takes the curse off Fewtrell in return for the candle trade, they are set for life. More importantly, "magic must close its ranks or vanish." Married, they'd have the market cornered on magic. He finally wins Benoni by telling her there is more to marriage than four bare legs in a blanket, her own remark to Bronwen. Benoni begins to laugh.

Davies concludes his Preface to *A Jig for the Gypsy* by a comment on the union of Benoni and the Conjuror. His romance, he says, is not intended in the "humourless" sense of a Hollywood film, nor is the play a realistic one: "The marriage of Benoni and the Conjuror is a union of two people of extraordinary character and outlook, as a defence against a world which is becoming more and more unfriendly toward their kind." Benoni was trapped only in the world of politics, not in her own world of "nature and magic."

Davies' third Salterton novel, *A Mixture of Frailties*, ends with a similar union, this time of artists, as the young singer Monica Gall resolves to marry the famous English conductor, middle-aged Benedict Domdaniel.

Benoni, Conjuror Jones, and Jack the Skinner drink to the union: "The magic forever." Jack says it is like a wedding of the ancient gods, and Jones, that it has the firmest foundation for a marriage: joint interest. Despite such practical talk, the attraction is obviously and ironically a personal one. They marry by leaping over the broom hand in hand, and the play ends with the three laughing and singing and dancing, heedless of the rising storm.

"There's nothing tragic that doesn't have a comedy side, even when it's rough comedy." The words are Jesse Bramhall's, in "Brothers in the Black Art." This is a rough comedy, in Jesse's words, or black comedy, to use the fashionable critical term from the sixties. It is a tale of honour and friendship and love — and their opposites. A tale of suicide and of very ironic success. It was produced on CBC television on February 14, 1974, as part of a series of one-hour plays by Canadian writers entitled "The Play's the Thing" under Executive Producer Fletcher Markel. Sean Sullivan acted the part of the octogenarian Jesse, and John Friesen, Jesse Junior. It has not yet been published. Davies draws on his own and his father's long experience in printing and publishing for much of the background of this play.

The Black Art is the printing business, a genuine craft in the nineteenth century when the play begins, one calling for judgment and artistry. The Black Art also becomes, as the full import of the play turns over in our minds, the mysterious art of love and friendship. Perhaps, too, the art of living. A black-and-white pattern of contrasts runs through the play. This colour symbolism suggests the tensions involved in loving and living, and the opposite types of behaviour illustrated by Evvy and Bess, or by Jesse, Griff and Phil. The printers have white hands from the lye used in the craft for washing the forms and the type. After a year, a man's hands stayed white for life. The printers were called The Lily-White Boys because of it, Jesse laughs. They gloried in the name. Black ink, white hands. (Pure hands, and a clean heart?) The colour pattern is picked up at the time of Phil's suicide, when his mouth is seen as a ruinous black hole in the midst of a stone-white face. The same lye which whitened his hands has blackened his mouth and throat, and taken his life.

The play begins with an old typographer being interviewed by a newspaper reporter, a young woman to whom the man of nearly ninety enjoys talking. But Jesse is really talking to his dead and much-beloved wife Bess. Senator Owen Griffiths has just died. He and Jesse were apprentice printers together, many years ago, and the reporter wants Jesse to say something about the Senator's early days, long before he got to be a publisher, a cabinet minister, and finally a senator. The scene cuts to show a winter funeral in Ottawa, complete with off-key band, as Jesse thinks out loud about Griff's funeral and about the kind of winter funerals Canada puts on for her great men: "Vincent Massey, General Vanier, Lester Pearson, all buried on bitter cold days in falling snow. Mourners in fur coats and hats. The band a bit out of tune because the instruments are cold."[5] Jesse's mind has moved back to the days when he and Griff were journeymen printers. Another cut, to show the Labour Day parade and the contest for Best-Dressed Union won by their Local in 1899, 1900 and 1901. The white hands of the marchers touch off the explanation about ink and lye. Jesse shows the reporter a colour photograph of the Senator, his hands noticeably white. The portrait is inscribed "For Jesse from Griff — Brothers in the Black Art." The play's original opening, before Davies revised it, showed Jesse being interviewed on his ninetieth birthday as the oldest member of the International Typographical Union in Canada. Griff's death is mentioned more casually as having taken place a few years earlier. The two versions converge on the photo with its curious inscription.

The scene moves to the printing shop, circa 1898, where Griff, a new man, is being knocked about by an old-timer for a careless error. The language is lively — a bit too lively for the CBC, as revisions indicate, but Davies manages to retain the colourful and authentic printer's slang: *screamer*, *shriek-mark*, *belly-cheat*, etc. This is a fine bit of comedy, and makes a nice contrast with the romantic mood of the winter funeral.

The three young apprentices — Jesse, Griff, and a young man called Phil — become friends. Cut to a scene where the high-spirited youths are cycling through the countryside, "all drunk and wild with youth and poetry." They declaim loudly as they ride, revelling in the melodramatic and tragic lines of poetry, until they run into some cows.

Five years pass. The three are now full journeymen, each with their girls. Griff's girl Lou, ironically termed the New Woman by Jesse, is a little like Boy

Staunton's second wife in *Fifth Business*, but not so nasty. Jesse loves a musician called Bess. Phil has fallen for Evvy, a beautiful young girl from the wrong side of town whom the Brotherhood distrust. "I don't think Evvy's quite straight" is the most charitable way that Bess can put it.

Lou, the intellectual of the group, quotes a visiting clergyman: "We may tell much — perhaps everything — about a man's character if we observe in what guise he invites beauty to touch his life." Beauty for Jesse is embodied in Bess's whole being and their life together. Beauty for Griff means music, and those, as he puts it, who are worthy of music. The fact that the Senator stopped singing as he moved into wealth and fame sets his success in an ironic light, although Jesse, who does not seem to resent the Senator's neglect of old friends as he moves up the social ladder, says that it's all rubbish to say that success and wealth cannot be reconciled with happiness. Beauty for young Elmo Gould means the theatre; he is fond of telling anyone who will listen that he has seen Irving six or seven times.

Beauty for Phil, as he tells his two friends, means "Evvy, and just Evvy, and nobody and nothing in the world else but Evvy." He is not afraid of Beauty: "We'll be a long time dead. While I live, I'll live as intensely and as truly as I know how." The two have not been married long before a flash photo of a naked bathing party, three men and three girls, is circulating in the printing shop. One of the girls is Evvy. (The photo is shown on screen. The stage directions describe it in some detail, ending: "The effect of the picture is artless and rather absurd, but plainly the subjects think themselves perfect devils.") The friends are at a loss as to how to tell Phil, but before they have decided what to do, he is found dead in the urinal. And Evvy has disappeared.

Evvy, as the young girl from the slums with her eye on the main chance, contrasts well both with Bess's solid worth and with the idealistic Phil. The youth's unrealistic and reverential attitudes (he looks upon Evvy as a saint and himself as unworthy of her) parody Victorian sensibilities and the Victorian tendency to put woman on a pedestal. One of Phil's favourite pictures is of a duel, entitled "For He Had Spoken Lightly of a Woman's Name." Going to bed with him, Evvy remarks scornfully, is like High Mass on Easter Sunday: "All this *sacred joy*."

The full story of what drove Phil to suicide is reserved for the end of the play, when Evvy encounters Jesse in the Exhibition Grounds in the summer of 1924. Evvy, now remarried, looks youthful and prosperous. Her speech has improved, although the old slang returns as she talks. She taunts Jesse with Griff's success and his neglect of Jesse. She always hated the Brothers in the Black Art and their mutual admiration society. It comes through indirectly that the Brothers stood for something — call it honour — which galled the girl from the slums: "All noble and knights of old and 'how-dare-you, you bastard.' God, Jesse, wake up; you were just a bunch of journeymen printers."

Evvy tells Jesse of Phil's last night: of his unexpected return from the night-shift, his discovery of his wife in bed with George Harrison, and their fight. Harrison won, and Phil left the house crying, thinking that it was all Harrison's fault and that he was incapable of defending his wife. Evvy and Harrison took the night train to Detroit; he left her, she tells Jesse, ten days later. She didn't brood; she learned. What she has learned, obviously, is to hide her past very successfully and play the middle-class matron to perfection. She is very solicitous about the morality of her adolescent children.

The last scene returns us to Jesse with the girl reporter as he sums up what the Brothers in the Black Art wanted out of life: love, honour, and beauty in her many guises.

The play offers a wide range of moods and some highly dramatic scenes. The wedding, with Evvy opening the modest gifts like a little girl under a Christmas tree and the depressed friends feeling that Phil is making a dreadful mistake by marrying Evvy, combines comedy with just the right amount of pathos. Evvy's crassness is revealed in a scene with Jesse in the Exhibition Grounds as she interrupts her story of Phil being beaten by Harrison to ask for another of Jesse's Chinese Chews or to mock Phil's taste in pictures. The discovery of Phil's dead body in the washroom of the printing shop is a powerful scene. We feel, with the printers, the horror of the act, and the mute desperation of the man who committed it. The flashbacks move back and forth smoothly over a seventy-year span. Jesse, like Margaret Laurence's ninety-year-old Hagar, is a man of sufficient depth and force to make an excellent central focus for the drama.

The technique of "Leaven of Malice," subtitled A Theatrical Extravaganza, is unlike any of Davies' other plays. There is no formal scenery and a minimum of props. Scenes change rapidly from one locale to another, often simply by means of lighting, with surprising ease and fluidity. It is no easy task to transform a long novel into a successful play, but Davies has succeeded brilliantly.[6]

The plot follows that of the novel, centering on a fictitious engagement announcement in the Salterton *Evening Bellman*, the local newspaper. Professor Vambrace, the father of Pearl, and Mrs. Bridgetower, the mother of the man named in the announcement are outraged, since they are old antagonists. The young pair do not know one another, and Solly Bridgetower fancies himself in love with a different girl. The comedy revolves around the put-down of the domineering parents (a comic treatment of the Oedipus theme), the blossoming of love between the two named in the announcement, and the unravelling of the mystery of who maliciously put the notice in the paper.

There are three acts and a multiplicity of short scenes. The lights come up on Gloster Ridley, editor of the *Bellman*. He is dressed in doctoral robes and stands before a dimly perceived academic group. His formal Convocation speech, thanking the university for the honorary doctorate he has been given in recognition of his services on behalf of the new Faculty of Journalism, defines a newspaper as a barber's chair which fits all buttocks. Ridley steps forward while his academic robes are held in place by masked figures like the operators of the Japanese puppet theatre. Wearing an ordinary business suit, Ridley addresses the audience in a confidential manner. His persona or public mask has been shed with his academic robe, which continues to have an existence of its own. In the dream sequence at the end of Act Two, the doctoral cap and gown worn by a masked figure advances to meet Ridley. The editor converses with the cap and gown, which nods and shrugs in reply.

In the novel, Ridley never acquires the honorary degree and has ceased to lust after it by the end. The play begins in the following year and moves back to the events of the preceding autumn (i.e. the events of the novel). While Ridley is making his confidential disclosure to the audience, that newspaper life is not simply as described in his Convocation address, the academic figures disappear and their place is taken by a triple charade which sums up much of the action of the play. A furious Professor Vambrace is mocked by Humphrey Cobbler; Solomon Bridgewater and Pearl Vambrace embrace; and the Professor strikes Pearl with a heavy stick and drives Solly away. The audience is thus shown, in the silent action of a few minutes, the puzzling and intriguing events which Ridley proposes to clarify. The incidents that lay behind these events, he adds, very nearly kept him from getting the handsome scarlet robe he has just acquired.

The play also uses large printed signs. The engagement notice is carried on stage as Pearl reads it in the newspaper; and Mrs. Bridgetower's portion of the dream sequence includes a similar sign depicting an engraved wedding invitation to the marriage of Solly and his mother. Marcel Marceau's mimes are announced by large signs carried by an elegant and colourful figure, but Davies' signs are carried by masked figures like the puppeteers of Japanese *bunraku*.

The next two scenes use spotlights to suggest people phoning one another from different houses. The confusion and ill-feeling caused by the announcement continues to spread. Professor Vambrace's rudeness to the Dean is purely comic; his browbeating of Pearl, blackly so. Mrs. Bridgetower, whom the Dean describes as his cross, insists that the Dean investigate the irreligious sounds she hears coming from the Cathedral.

The Cathedral scene is one of the best in the play. Organist Humphrey Cobbler, an irrepressible and unconventional spirit, is celebrating Hallowe'en with some masked and costumed students from the University Glee Club. Cobbler and students taunt Vambrace, who is looking for the Dean, with an irreverent song, until the Dean enters in cassock and pyjamas. Just a Hallowe'en prank, Cobbler apologizes. Even God enjoys a good time now and again. The organ is drawn offstage with Cobbler cheerfully improvising on it as Ridley and his housekeeper enter for the next scene. Similarly, the characters of the following scene are heard talking in the wings before Ridley has quitted the stage. The pace is brisk.

Solly and Pearl drive onstage in Solly's little car. They discuss the horrors of the Yarrows' party, from which they have just come. We are switched back to the time of the party. This affair, where couples are tied together and left to wriggle free, is not as funny as it is in the novel. But the Yarrows are a precious pair. Norm Yarrow is a guidance counsellor at the university. His speech reeks of the jargon of his profession. Norm describes Pearl as "a shy kiddie, brainy, not the aggressive type." He is not sure whether or not her life has yet found its Faith Focus, where doubts and fears are sublimated in that vast Power about whose vastness and sublimity he and his wife feel themselves supremely qualified to speak. The best that Norm can wish for Solly and Pearl is a fulfillment of their Affection Potential such as he and his wife enjoy.

Act Three shows the Yarrows in bed together enjoying a game of toesies and commiserating with one another about Pearl and Solly's troubles. This is followed by Yarrow bearding Professor Vambrace in his study to inform him of his Oedipal attitude towards his daughter. Since Vambrace holds the Chair of Classics at the University, he *is* familiar with the story of Oedipus. Yarrow is a little slow to realize this, but not displeased when he does: "It's always easier in these problems of Relationship Engineering when we have to deal with a man of intelligence." The mention of incest upsets the counsellor. Not real incest, he says, just mental incest. Nothing serious. This sets Vambrace up for a marvellous line, a truth of which latter-day puritans need to be reminded: "Do you suggest that the sins of the mind are trivial, whereas the sins of the flesh are important? What kind of an idiot are you?" Vambrace finally squelches Yarrow, calling him an aspiring Sphinx, "an under-educated, brassy young pup, who thinks that gall can take the place of the authority of wisdom, and that professional lingo can disguise his lack of thought." He drives Yarrow from his office, then collapses in tears, murmuring "Pearl."

Scenes continue to change rapidly. At one point the stagehands are moving furniture during the action. And one character, reluctant to give up the limelight, tries to continue talking while the characters of the next scene are waiting to begin. The actors finally call upon the stage manager for assistance, and the garrulous character is comically carried from the stage by masked figures.

Act Two includes a parody of Eliot's verse-drama (not so farcical as the parody in *A Masque of Mr. Punch*) and a wonderful scene in the Cobblers' bedroom. Humphrey is laid low with a bad head cold, a two-sheet cold, as he puts it. (He prefers to blow his nose in old bedsheets.) Solly comes with a bottle of rye, a Greek bearing gifts. Cobbler convinces Solly, through a series of rhetorical questions asked by Cobbler and loyally answered by Molly that he was not the one who put the announcement in the newspaper.[7] The bedroom fades into a scene between Solly and Higgin (a recent British immigrant who teaches music and elocution, or speech engineering, as he prefers to call it in the New World), then back to the bedroom. Solly tells the Cobblers a comi-pathetic tale of how he has been stuck with Charles Heavysege as his thesis topic. Cobbler advises Solly to *create*. Write a novel. Stop thinking of himself as a toad under the harrow. By this time Solly is tucked into the foot of the Cobblers' bed, with his feet up towards them. The three fall asleep, and a five-part dream sequence follows.

This sequence illustrates Shaw's remark that there is a musical counterpart for much of what happens in a good play. Davies uses musical terms to suggest the mood of each dream. Mrs. Bridgetower's dream of marrying her son is to be played *andante con tenerezza*. Ridley's conversation with the cap and gown of his honorary degree is *grave e misterioso*; Higgin's earlier life and his frustrated ambitions are expressed *religioso, teneramente*; Professor Vambrace's dream of Pearl, and of nobility and security, is *appasionamente*; and Molly Cobbler's dream of her husband and their life together is *con amore*.

The whodunit mystery is resolved in a dramatic scene in Ridley's office near the end of the play. The culprit is Higgin, a nasty and pathetic little man who felt he had been snubbed by each of the parties whom the announcement was intended to hurt: Ridley, Solly, Pearl, and the elderly journalist Shillito. Discovered, Higgin weeps like a child: "You people don't know what it's like to come to a new country, which everybody says is so free, and find yourself in a town like this that's so close, so snug, so forbidding, so denying." Higgin's inflated opinion of himself has been the basis of several comic scenes. Now we find his discomfiture genuinely moving. As the Dean puts it, we often do very stupid and wicked things and don't know why. The Dean quotes from the Anglican Prayer Book a prayer that we be preserved from the leaven of malice and wickedness, adding: "Malice may well be called a leaven; it transforms whatever it touches . . . . There is no one of us here who has not been changed and tainted by the leaven of malice during this past week."

Vambrace, unappeased, is still for sueing the newspaper, but Solly and Pearl have something to tell him. The Cobblers guess what it is, and Humphrey shouts like a schoolboy: Solomon Bridgetower loves Pearl Vambrace. Solly, in the comic metaphor of the play, is the metamorphosed Frog Prince, no longer a toad under the harrow. The play ends in the traditional manner of comedy, with a wedding procession. The stage fills with rosy light, cupids and marriage garlands are projected at the back, and the cast pairs off in a wedding dance. Ridley dances with his doctoral gown (masked figure within), and Vambrace is comically paired with his old antagonist, Mrs. Bridgetower. The music is "This is the way to the zoo," the song which Cobbler used earlier to taunt Professor Vambrace, played now with country-dance simplicity.

Notes to Chapter 4

1. See, for example, George Bernard Shaw, *Major Barbara* and *Mrs. Warren's Profession*. In the latter play, the extremely conventional Praed poses as an anarchist, while Vivie Warren, daughter of a high-class madam, is all common sense and practicality. In his Preface to *Major Barbara*, Shaw speaks of the respect which society accords to the successful scoundrel.

2. In *Fortune, My Foe*, Nicholas says that revolutions never change anything that matters: "they merely put power in new hands, and the new masters have to serve their apprenticeship to civilization, like the rulers they have overthrown . . . . The only revolutions that make any real difference to the world are revolutions in the hearts of individual men." Robertson Davies, *Four Favorite Plays* (Clarke, Irwin, 1968), p.134.

3. Margaret Atwood bases the ending of her 1974 television drama about a servant girl in Upper Canada upon the interest which Susanna Moodie was known to have had in phrenology.

4. Davies' remark constitutes a dig at Mackenzie King, who consulted fortune tellers and believed that he was in touch with the spirit of his deceased mother.

5. Bits of actual films of the state funerals of General Vanier and Lester Pearson were used.

6. When the play ran at the Martin Beck Theatre in New York under the title "Love and Libel," Walter Kerr found it "a curious series of oddball musings from the mind of an obviously sophisticated man" (*Herald Tribune*, 8 December 1960); and Robert Coleman wrote: "Satiric thrusts alternate with blunt broadsides . . . . There's too much corn for good comedy" (*New York Mirror*, 8 December 1960).

   This critique is based upon a 1973 typescript of the play lent to me by the author and has no necessary bearing on the Summer 1975 production at Niagara-on-the-Lake, which I did not see. Reviewing this production in *The Globe and Mail*, Clive Barnes quoted the following line as 'typical' of the play: "There's more to marriage than four bare legs under a blanket." Since this line belongs originally in Davies' *A Jig for the Gypsy*, one wonders whether this and possibly other alterations were the work of the author or the producer.

7. Example: "'They are bourgeois; I am an artist. And therein lies my defence. Can you conceive of any practical joke more tiresomely bourgeois, more quintessentially and ineluctably middle class, than shoving a fake engagement notice in the paper?' Molly: 'No!'"

5

Breaching the Barrier Between Actor and Audience: Davies' Masques

The masque form, like drama itself, probably originated in primitive religious rites. It appears in many societies, in varying forms. Masques frequently culminate in an impromptu dance involving both spectators and performers. In England, the masque developed through thinly disguised fertility rites such as the St. George "Sword Dance" folk plays, and in elaborate court entertainments in the sixteenth and seventeenth centuries. During the reign of James I (1603-1625) and his pleasure-loving wife Anne, and in the hands of Ben Jonson and the architect Inigo Jones, the masque became an ornate and elaborate spectacle.

Davies acknowledges Jonson as an influence on his drama.[1] Jonson wrote twenty-five masques. The masque tradition that he inherited emphasized song and dance, and had little dramatic weight. Jonson gave it a substantial poetic and literary framework, and introduced the anti-masque, a comic interlude which parodied the major plot. Davies has written two masques for performance by the boys of Upper Canada College Preparatory School, *A Masque of Aesop* and *A Masque of Mr. Punch*. Although indebted to the masque tradition and, as Davies suggests, to Jonson, these plays are also thoroughly contemporary and Canadian. This is especially true of the second masque, written in the early sixties.

In his book on the Jonsonian masque, Stephen Orgel objects to the masque being defined primarily by the culminating dance in which both actors and audience join. Some masques involve no dancing whatsoever. Orgel locates the critical feature of the masque not in form but in function, in an unique kind of relationship between its action and audience. The masque attempted to breach the barrier between spectators and actors, so that in effect the viewer became part of the spectacle: "The end toward which the masque moved was to destroy any sense of theatre and to include the whole court in the mimesis—in a sense, what the spectator watched he ultimately became."[2] The revels were a means, but not the only means, to this end.

Davies' masques are primarily satiric and comic. They are largely anti-masques, the term given to the satiric or grotesque interludes which Jonson set against his more usual, light-hearted matter. In his Introduction to *A Masque of Aesop* (1952), Davies speaks of the freedom from conventional form which is permitted in the masque entertainment. The first freedom which the playwright has pre-empted is the mixture of Greek and Roman names for the ancient gods. Davies simply chose whichever name was currently popular and more likely to be known to his audience.

A Masque of Aesop Davies' first masque is built around Apollo's encounter with Aesop and a mob of irate citizens. The handsome, dignified Apollo is the god of music, the arts, and agriculture. He is also, as he reminds us, the god who watches over the affairs of boys, hence particularly suitable to this occasion. The setting is the facade of Apollo's Temple at Delphi. In line with the masque tradition of spectacle, there are richly coloured draperies and an Empyraeum or heaven, a blue cloth spangled with stars: the Inigo Jones touch. Apollo's aunts, the Parcae or Fates, are three disreputable and sharp-tongued hags. Apollo and the Parcae set to work to draw spectators and actors together. The Parcae demand to be introduced to Apollo's "stylish friends," alias the audience. Their banter makes it clear that family squabbles are common to men and gods alike. Davies' implication that myth is living history comes through Apollo's comic revelation that Hippocrates, Juno, Vulcan, Venus and Colonel Mars are living members of the audience.

Enter the mob, dragging Aesop in a large sack. The rest of the masque consists of the mob's condemnation of Aesop, and his trial by Apollo. The god permits Aesop to stage three of his favourite tales as evidence, and as defence against the mob's judgment that he deserves to die. The three playlets, or anti-masques, show that a successful life involves inner peace and self-knowledge. This is also a theme in Davies' fiction, especially in *The Manticore*. The masque's final mood, captured in a hymn and a slow procession, is one of dignity and solemnity after the farce and slapstick comedy of the anti-masques.

Aesop's attempt to tell the truth has provoked the citizens. The editor of the most widely circulated journal in Delphi says he has first publication rights to the truth. The leading priest objects to Aesop's criticism, and the representative of organized labour calls Aesop an unsettling influence: "unless society is reasonably stable my followers cannot threaten it with the horrors of instability." The citizens insist that real entertainment is "harmless and improving."

Aesop's first offering in his own defence is called "The Belly and the Members." Needless to say, the good bourgeois object to the title and suggest that *abdomen* should be substituted for *belly*. Appollo advises them that really nice people use whatever language they choose and thereby dignify it.[3] Aesop's players are the Head, Right Hand, Left Hand, Right Leg, Left Leg, Heart, Belly, and an Unidentified Part which turns out to be the rump. Davies had already used the concept of the body as a government bureaucracy in his first play, *Eros at Breakfast*. Each of the members considers itself the most important part of the body politic. They attempt to rebel against the Belly and find themselves dependent upon it. The Belly draws the moral. They are like a great country divided into many provinces. Each insists upon its rights, but all are dependent on a central government: "Would it not be wise, therefore, to behave like interdependent provinces, rather than wrangling and opposed independent states?" The Unidentified Part is the sat-upon taxpayer. The anti-masque closes with a comic song. Strength is born of union and "nations, when quarrels rot 'em/must build up from the bottom." The citizens are pleased with the moral, until Aesop adds that it refers not only to unity within a country but to world unity as well. This leads to fresh dissension. Appollo asks for Aesop's second play, "The Town Mouse and the Country Mouse."

Davies version of this popular fable is a delight. The mice sing several songs with highly comic rhymes, and engage in a farcical dialogue. Their friendship, touted as "greasy,/gelatinous, thick and gluey," is also deathless and calm: "Depressive? No, nor manic,/But Pythias and Damonic/And David and Jonathanic."

The dandified town mouse invites his country friend to his sixteen-room mansion, "infested" with humans. He aspires to make a mouse-about-town of his unkempt country cousin. They sit down to a banquet but are interrupted by a cat ten feet high and twenty-five feet long: the grotesque element in the anti-masque tradition. The town mouse says to expect this two or three times a meal. The country mouse declares that humble fare enjoyed in peace is preferable to guilty and uneasy splendour. He sings and dances, using his string-tied umbrella as a partner.

Some citizens consider the fable to be an attack on rural life, and others, a sneer at urban civilization: "Haven't we got a subway? What more could even a mouse demand?" (The Toronto north-south subway had just been built in 1952.) Aesop says his fable was "only intended to suggest that peace of mind is an agreeable possession." The Fates support him, adding that no one has peace of mind until he has come to terms with himself.

"The Cock and the Pearl" has the most vulgar characters, the most farcical dialogue, and the sharpest satire of the three anti-masques. The Cock is inspecting his family, military style, and catechizing them. To questions such as "What are we going to do today?" and "What is the beginning and end of all wisdom?" his Chicks and Hen return the proper answer: "Keep an eye on the

Main Chance.'' Satisfied, the Cock says he will give the sun ''leave to rise upon another day of practical, down-to-earth, shoulder-to-the-wheel, nose-to-the-grindstone living.'' This comical collection of clichés recurs as a refrain. The Cock sings his scorn for art, philosophy and Romance and fobs off further questions from the Chicks by advising them that their answers will be found in a few words in Breeder's Digest, Creeder's Digest, and Bleeder's Digest.

Breakfast time is an occasion for giving thanks for living in a world where everything can be swallowed without questioning. After the Cock has choked on something, the Pearl rolls out of the food basket and unfolds herself, calm and beautiful. To the Cock and his family, the Pearl is obviously an inedible piece of grit. Is she good for children, the Hen enquires? She serves only to awaken them to beauty. The Cock's family knows that beauty consists of their celluloid leg rings. They sum up the Pearl as useless and unwholesome, simply ''grit you can't eat.'' The citizens consider it an attack upon vocational education. Aesop's dictum that a man who knows nothing but his job is not fit to be a citizen provokes charges of blasphemy and calls for his death.

Apollo rebukes the citizens for their blindness and Aesop for the arrogance of his wisdom: perfect wisdom is an attribute of the gods alone. Apollo decrees that Aesop's fables will delight children for centuries to come, but only the wisest will remember and interpret them when childhood is past: ''For the greatest teacher is he who has passed through scorn of mankind, to love of mankind.''

Ben Jonson satirized hypocrisy, stupidity, greed, and self-importance. The title of his last comedy, *The Devil is an Ass* (1616), suggests that the devil is a piker compared to mankind. Davies is obviously after similar game, even in these light entertainments.

A Masque of Mr. Punch (1963) draws on another tradition and on the hero and heroine of countless English puppet shows. In the traditional story, Punch kills his infant child and bludgeons his wife to death; is imprisoned; escapes; encounters and outwits several characters, including the Devil.[4] Davies' first version (his masque contains two Punch and Judy shows) has Judy and the baby surviving, while the Hangman is a victim of his own noose, and the Doctor, of his own medicine. At the end of Davies' masque, Mephistopheles pronounces Punch to be ''the Spirit of Unregenerate Man,'' and the Old Adam, without whom the human race would cease to be human.

Davies writes that Mr. Punch has been an influence on him since he first, as a small boy, saw a Punch and Judy show: ''I have admired and coveted his gaiety, his masterful way with physical and metaphysical enemies, and his freedom from remorse. As a literary influence Mr. Punch is neither classic nor romantic, but demonic, without a parallel in life or art.''[5] Something of Punch's gaiety, his demonic energy and his mocking of bourgeois morality is caught in the figure of Humphrey Cobbler, the bohemian church organist in the Salterton novels.

The structural framework in this masque with a contemporary setting, involves the news media, a public relations man, drama critics and playwrights. The spectators are likely to find their own attitudes depicted and mocked in these characters, whose farcical incomprehension of the Punch and Judy show has the effect of increasing the audience's enjoyment of it. This is a useful device, for without such a framework some, at least, of Davies' spectators might react to Punch as do the solemn critics. We see, in effect, our prejudices acted out on stage.

The opening lines of the media people, spoken in a portentous manner, contribute a parody of a Greek chorus and, specifically, of several passages in T.S. Eliot's verse drama, *Murder in the Cathedral*. They describe themselves as the flower of Canadian journalism. Condemned to wait, they suffer the actions of others, "thinking, and partly thinking — /Assured that *Time* will explain, and *Life* illustrate in full colour,/All that man knows about earth, or needs to know of the heavens." The Morning-Paper Critic, clearly a snob, uses self-conscious academic rhetoric, while the language of the Evening-Paper Critic and the Television Man and Woman is colloquial and vulgar: "where's the booze?" The setting is an ugly Victorian hotel room. They are awaiting a distinguished visitor from Europe called, variously, M. Polichinelle, Signor Punchinello, and Mr. Punch. What's his program, they ask, his sponsor and his preferred public image?

Punch and Judy are heard quarreling offstage, and the figure of a baby is flung violently across the stage before they enter. Punch copes with the infant's squalls by swinging it around by its feet while claiming to have taught Dr. Spock everything he knows. Punch greets the reporters, who proceed to tell him he is out of date. The Television Woman is impressed by the fact that Punch makes up his lines extempore. She considers this avant garde: "Gets rid of the author, which is always an important beginning to any serious work in the theatre." The media people suspect that Punch's notion of theatre is vulgar, a remark which Punch takes as a compliment. He offers to do his show, if some "real people" can be found for an audience. The newsmen are no help here, being accustomed to a captive audience, so Punch beats the drum himself, drawing schoolboys and groups of ladies and gentlemen. There are now "spectators" on stage, mingling with the other actors. A second backdrop, representing a seventeenth-century street, creates the stage within a stage for Punch's first show.

The antics in Punch's show include Punch's giving a pepper sandwich to dog Toby, being beaten by neighbour Harlequin, and throwing his baby into the sky when it refuses to stop howling. Baby's articles of clothing descend, one by one, at intervals as the play proceeds. Punch flirts with Polly the nursemaid and is beaten by Judy. A doctor is called for, and, after some horseplay, Punch jabs him with his own enormous syringe. A policeman accuses Punch of killing his baby, but Punch bribes the officer, father of seventeen, with an offer to buy one of his babies. The hangman is disposed of by being persuaded to demonstrate his trade secrets and the working of his rope, Tickler. Baby falls out of the sky, and Punch and Judy dance and sing. When a Devil appears, accompanied by flame and thunder, Punch stoutly insists upon his innocence. They fight. Punch beats him and proclaims "the Devil is dead!" The spectators on stage applaud, and an usher from the theatre audience presents Judy with a bouquet of vegetables, effecting a union of audience and actors.

Davies returns us to the comedy of the structural frame which holds the two anti-masques. The onstage spectators are incapable of expressing any opinions of Punch's show until they have been told what to think by an Adjudicator. This worthy declares the show to be an unsuccessful excursion into the Theatre of the Absurd, an exploration of the fragmentation of life and the despair which every intelligent contemporary theatregoer feels. The first part of the Adjudicator's speech is a parody of Sartre's ideas and of plays such as *No Exit*. The Adjudicator compliments Punch on his depiction of Freudian jealousy of the child and of the sadism which lurks behind the bourgeois façade. He also admires Punch's mockery of established institutions, in the manner of Brecht. But the dénouement, the death of the Devil, is utterly unacceptable to the Adjudicator. He suggests that the play be rewritten to give the Devil a bigger part and make him the hero. (Slapstick here, as the devil cheers and is knocked down again by Punch.) As for the happy ending, the Adjudicator finds it intolerable: "We shall not build an indigenous Canadian theatre on plays with happy endings. We are miserable or we are nothing. Hope is out of fashion."

Two modern playwrights offer to rewrite Punch's show. Davies thereby satirizes several contemporary schools of drama, and illustrates the kind of thing the Adjudicator would be pleased to see. The representative of American Southern Decadence would turn Punch into a southern belle and set the action in a decaying family mansion in a swamp: Punch slinks provocatively across the stage, draped in a cloak. A character called Samuel Bucket, avant garde European dramatist, envisages the show in terms of the Theatre of the Absurd. The action would consist of two garbage cans in an alley, one empty, one containing Punch. The lid would be securely wired down, and the "comedy" would consist of nothing whatsoever happening for three-quarters of an hour, as Punch struggled to communicate with the other garbage can: "*No* is the dominant symbol of the play." Davies' Bucket is an amusing parody of the Irish dramatist Samuel Beckett, whose drama and fiction portrays human helplessness and frustration. Anyone who is familiar with Beckett's *Endgame* (1957) or *Happy Days* (1961) will appreciate the joke. In *Endgame*, the anti-hero Hamm is blind and chair-bound, while his parents Nagg and Nell are confined to garbage cans. Winnie, in *Happy Days*, is embedded in sand to her waist.

A new interpreter steps forward, a professor who claims that Punch's show was presented with the wrong emphasis. It is really a tragedy, "a great revelation of the human spirit under stress.'' The professor, representing the Board of Governors of the Stratford Shakespearean Festival, offers to show Punch a Shakespearean version of his show. The second anti-masque follows, in the form of a hilarious and grotesque parody of an Elizabethan tragedy. There are obvious echoes of *Hamlet* and *Macbeth*. King Punch's heart is heavy, cankered with lust for Prince Omlet's rattle. Filled with *hubris*, and undeterred by the witch's prophecy of doom upon whomever steals the rattle, King Punch stabs in quick succession Queen Judy, the baby, and Paulina. Harlequin and Toby (''noblest of Dumb Chums'' and ''the doggedest dog in all dogdom'') drag the bodies from the stage. King Punch delivers a speech in the grand manner, about grim days, dark nights, and the murky horrors of his soul. The ghosts of Queen Judy, Pauline and Prince Omlet enter and claim the rattle. King Punch recovers his spirit, and fights the Devils until he loses his reason in the manner of Ophelia. He expires, mourned by the Second Devil in a parody of lines stolen from Christopher Marlow's *Dr. Faustus*: ''Cut is the branch that might have grown full straight,/And Punch will never see St. Peter's gate.'' He is carried off while the orchestra plays the Dead March and guns are fired offstage.

The real Punch has no use for this version. He objects to the ending, where the devil beats Punch: ''The whole point of Punch's Show is that nobody beats Punch.'' The media people are unimpressed by both versions and dismiss Punch as a thoughtless entertainment from a naïve era. Punch is vindicated by Mephistopheles, a very superior devil, who says that humanity cannot spare Punch. Without him, mankind will soon be living on government pensions and grants. Punch, in other words, is the spirit of youth and daring and laughter. The Spirit of Unregenerate Man. Mephistopheles suggests that Punch try his hand at politics: ''It's full of Judys to be bullied, Tobys to be bribed and coaxed to jump through hoops, doctors to be given doses of their own medicines, officers to be swindled, and hangmen to be tricked. Are you game?'' The world is Punch's oyster. The masque ends with a song celebrating the world as Punch's Show.

The Shakespearean version of Punch is a choice example of comic bathos, and an exquisite parody of Elizabethan tragedy. The demonic gaiety of the original Mr. Punch pervades the entire masque, and Mephistopheles' final speech drives home the relevance of Punch to actors and audience alike. The range of other dramatists and various types of drama parodied here, from Shakespeare to T.S. Eliot and Samuel Beckett, is remarkable for a short play.

Davies' masques dramatize an image of society and draw the audience into it. Human folly and vanity and pretensions are exposed, through laughter, and a vision of beauty and of a desirable society is revealed. As in the Elizabethan masque, the forms of art become metaphors for the social forms we call manners: ''The viewer . . . having experienced the masque, is himself capable of dancing.''[6]

Notes to Chapter Five

1. See Samuel Marchbanks, "The Double Life of Robertson Davies," Carl F. Klinck and Reginald Watters, eds., *Canadian Anthology* (Toronto: Gage, 1966), p.399.

2. Stephen Orgel, *The Jonsonian Masque* (Cambridge, Mass.: Harvard University Press,1965), pp.6-7.

3. Mark Twain described himself as a man who had always catered for the Belly and the Members. Davies, quoting Twain's letter, writes: "if ever a man wrote for the Belly and the Members, it was Leacock." See Robertson Davies, *Feast of Stephen. A Leacock Anthology* (Toronto: McClelland and Stewart, 1974), p.1.

4. See William Rose Benet, *The Reader's Encyclopedia*, Second Ed., Vol.I (New York: Thomas Cromwell,1965), p.826: "The irascible hump-backed, hook-nosed Punch is thought to be derived from Pulcinella, the slow-witted servant of the *commedia dell' arte*, who was also a great favorite in Italian puppet shows. By about 1650, this character was appearing in puppet shows in France; transformed into the witty Polichinelle reaching England at the time of the Restoration, he became known as Punchinello or Punch. In their present form, Punch and his wife Judy, who was originally called Joan, date from about 1800."

5. Robertson Davies, *A Masque of Mr. Punch* (Toronto: Oxford University Press,1963), Introduction, p.xi. Cf. Maurice Baring, *Punch and Judy and Other Essays* (London: Heinemann, 1924), pp.3-24. Baring notes that the eye quickly tires of the slavish realism of elaborate scenery, and that Punch and Judy provide "the opportunity of make-believe: and with the minimum of effort they achieved the maximum of effect" (p.18).

6. Orgel, *The Jonsonian Masque*, p.183.

6

'The Comedy Company of the Psyche'

General Confession (1956) is an ingenious dramatization of Jung's analytical psychology. The four major archetypes of the collective unconscious serve as the principal actors, and the Jungian goal of personal integration becomes the climax of the play. It is at the same time an excellent piece of theatre. The Comedy Company of the Psyche, as Davies called Jung's theory of the structure of personality in his novel *The Manticore*, is a concept which easily lends itself to dramatization. And where Jung's theories will not serve the dramatic purpose, the playwright does not hesitate to choose a dramatically effective scheme rather than the abstract concept. In the curtain line at the end of Act Two, Voltaire congratulates Casanova on "a unique experience in self-recognition." We are indebted to Davies for a unique experiment in showing us to ourselves.

The play is set in the summer of 1797, in the library of the castle residence of Count Waldstein. The Count's daughter Amalie is brought by a young officer of Napoleon's army into a small private room or cabinet which opens off the great library. It is the haunted part of the library, Amalie says, where her father claims to have had the frightening experience of meeting himself. This remark helps to set the play's tone, and proves to be prophetic of the main plot. The setting is to be mysterious, romantic and baroque.

Hugo's hope of seducing Amalie is upset by her sense of humour and his deficiency in this regard, whereupon the aged Casanova, the Count's librarian, reveals his presence in the gloom of the cabinet. He retains his lively interest in the technique of seduction and his sense of life as theatre, the most entrancing of plays, as he tells Amalie: "Ah, how many times have I not played the scene which you have just—may I say it?—bungled." Amalie then wishes to stay to talk with Casanova, who offers to entertain the lovers with neither the logic of music nor the bustling unreason of Italian comedy but simply with the tale of a man's life. Hugo's fear that the Librarian will play the dull lecturer and read from his memoirs, a thick manuscript on his desk, is a repeated comic motif.

The cabinet is lined with three special bookcases, where the Count keeps what Casanova calls the cynical, un-Christian philosophers (Voltaire chief among them); the magicians and alchemists; and erotic stories: a room, in short, of powerful and forbidden things. By the aid of some cabbalistic gibberish, Casanova proceeds to call up from the three bookcases the spirits of Voltaire, Cagliostro, and the Ideal Beloved.

Voltaire's education, comically, has been continuing since he quitted his human body. He tells the others that no one was more astonished than he to discover that there is indeed an afterlife. The Ideal Beloved is a mysterious beauty, masked and cloaked. Her presence restores Casanova's youth and he makes love to her using the same words that Hugo has used to Amalie. Repetition or parallelism is one of Davies' favourite comic techniques. Cagliostro is a figure of menace. Casanova recognizes him as an enemy, and the first act closes with their duel. The surreal nature of the play is clear by their bloodless transfixing of one another with swords.

Act Two contains three mini-plays, involving the characters whom Casanova has evoked. The actors call these episodes charades and assume in them an exaggerated acting style. We might call them masques or (in the case of the third one, where the situation is grotesque) anti-masques. Like the masque, these episodes draw the audience and the actors more closely together and thus drive home the psychological parable. The third act is another mock-drama, consisting of Casanova's trial. The charge is that Casanova has committed the seven cardinal sins. Amalie is judge, Cagliostro is the prosecutor, and the Ideal Beloved is the witness for the defence.

The theme, then, is the growth of self-knowledge and integration in the psyche, which is seen to be complex and to consist of different foci of such strength and personality as to be aptly compared with persons. By recognizing these structures within the psyche and by coming to terms with them, Casanova wins through to the state of individuation and wholeness which Jung describes as the goal of human life.

The allegory of the four main characters, as representatives of what Jung called the persona, the anima, the shadow, and the self, is emphasized at the end of Acts Two and Three. Voltaire describes the Ideal Beloved, Cagliostro, and himself as those without whom there could be no Casanova. He tells Casanova bluntly that they have been summoned from within himself. Casanova is naturally sceptical. He boasts of his self-knowledge and simple unity: "I stand alone." He remembers these three as specific individuals met with earlier in life. Voltaire, in arguing that they must have some form in order to be seen and known, and that it is therefore perfectly reasonable that they should resemble people whom Casanova has known, is actually voicing Jung's theory that the persons in our dreams are projections of our own fears and desires and attitudes. Seen from this angle, the episodes of the play are like dreams that Casanova might have.

After the three charades, Hugo identifies Voltaire as Casanova's wisdom or better judgement. Amalie identifies the Ideal Beloved as his ideal of woman-hood, while the footman Wenzel sees that Cagliostro is his bad luck, his contrary destiny, ''everything that says 'No' to a man.'' Act Three begins with the external characters — Hugo, Amalie, Wenzel — realizing with comic consternation that they are all similarly equipped. There are more such charac-ters, Voltaire insists, but ''a quorum of the principal shareholders'' is formed by Voltaire, Marina, and Cagliostro acting as Casanova's Wisdom, Inspira-tion, and Bosom Enemy. Casanova himself is romantically described by the Ideal Beloved as the Hero, led onward by herself. After the trial scene, in which Casanova makes a confession which is both general and personal, he begins to fear that these three may destroy him. Voltaire gently reminds him of the strange relation they bear to him. They are one with himself. They want nothing from him which he does not want from himself, and their only power is to show him himself from an unfamiliar point of view, ''like light falling through a prism.'' The prism image suggests the self-knowledge which a person should acquire. As the conscious mind grows, it becomes individualized and differ-entiated from others. Self-knowledge is necessary, Jung believed, to maintain or recover the wholeness with which we are born and which we tend to lose in the process of individuation.

Jung viewed the psyche, or the personality as a whole, as being composed of three levels: consciousness (organized by the ego), the personal unconscious, and the collective unconscious. The personal unconscious is the storehouse of memories, perceptions and experiences which arise out of our personal past. The collective unconscious—Jung's discovery and the most unique part of his theory — is a reservoir of latent or primordial images inherited from our common ancestral past. The archetypes or prototypes of the collective uncon-scious act as predispositions or potentialities for responding to experiences in the ways in which our ancestors did. There are as many archetypes, Jung wrote, as there are typical situations in human life. Among those which he identified and described are those of birth, death, power, magic, the hero, the trickster, God, the philosopher-king, the earth-mother, many natural objects, and man-made objects such as rings and weapons.[1]

Jung identified four archetypes as basic components of the psyche. He considered these four to be of special importance in shaping personality and behaviour. The *persona* is the mask or social façade, the public image which one turns to the world. The word is Latin for the mask used in drama. I have identified Casanova, as he shows himself to the other actors and to us, with the persona. The Ideal Beloved calls him the Hero, another archetype, but we should remember that he is this *in relation to her*. The *anima* is the feminine side of the male psyche; similarly, there is a masculine side to the female psyche which Jung calls the *animus*. This archetype has been developed by exposure to and interaction with the other sex for many generations. Jung describes it as an imprint or deposit of all the impressions ever made by women upon the male (or, conversely, by men upon the female) psyche. Casanova's Ideal Beloved appears as a veiled Turkish beauty, as a young Frenchwoman masquerading as an officer, and as a sulky English trollop. In the Charpillion episode, the *anima* figure has neither mystery nor high breeding but rather raw sexuality and cruelty. She repudiates Casanova, mocking him as middle-aged, bestriding him like a horse and flogging him about the stage. The scene, with its threat of castration, suggests the well-known brothel scene in Joyce's *Ulysses* with whoremistress Bella-Bello Cohen.[2] In Act Three, the Ideal Beloved is witness for the defence in Casanova's trial, where she reminds the court that his offences are the common condition of man and that everyone present is guilty of them. They have charged Casanova with the sin of being a man: ''and where all are guilty, who dares judge?''

Casanova's adversary, or shadow, is the most interesting of the lot. Jung describes the shadow as the most powerful and potentially the most dangerous of all the archetypes, the source of man's best and of his worst. It contains the more animal and instinctual side, the strongest emotions and insights, the springs of creativity. The shadow appears to us under the guise of a figure of our own sex. It is the dark side of our personality, of which we are often unaware. John Sanford, in *Dreams, God's Forgotten Language*, describes the shadow as our angry side, our weakness, our sickness, our primitiveness, our sensuality, our rebelliousness or inferiority, whatever we are afraid of in ourselves and reluctant to face.[3] The shadow is also a cultural phenonemon, representing the neglected and repressed part of the *zeitgeist* in which we share. Sanford interprets the Old Testament story of Jacob wrestling with the angel, or with God Himself, and demanding to be blessed, as an image of the Jungian concept of everyman's struggle with his shadow.

Cagliostro, dressed in black and white and described as a figure of menace, is Casanova's antagonist under many forms. He is the Turkish Pasha who prevents Casanova's union with Sophia, the cousin of Henriette who separates her from her beloved, the one who demands that the Charpillion incident be included, and the prosecutor at Casanova's trial who charges him with having committed the sins of pride, envy, anger, lechery, avarice, gluttony, and sloth. Jung believed that an individual must recognize and accept his shadow, allowing him to play a part in the totality of personality. Near the end of the play, Casanova kneels before Cagliostro and looks into his eyes, whereupon Cagliostro breaks his sword and throws away the pieces.[4] For the rest of the play, Casanova acts vitally alive and happy.

There was a historical Cagliostro, an Italian count whose real name was Guiseppe Balsamo (1743-1795). The count was a charlatan who posed as a man of rank and who duped the credulous with feats of magic and alchemy. He was implicated in the "diamond necklace affair," an eighteenth-century scandal involving Marie Antoinette and highly placed members of the French court. He was condemned to death by the Inquisition for heresy but his sentence was commuted to life imprisonment. By choosing this name for the shadow archetype, Davies cleverly suggests that the shadow is sinister, powerful, something of a charlatan, and imprisoned (in the body) for life.

The centre of personality, which administers and controls the whole psyche, Jung calls the *self*. This archetype of order and organization is different from our conscious ego. Jung arrived at this concept as a result of and after completing his investigation of the collective unconscious. He described the self as life's goal, "the completest expression of that fateful combination we call individuality . . . ."[5] Voltaire is addressed by Cagliostro as Stage Manager. He has had the benefit of extra-terrestial education, a witty stroke suggestive of the spiritual dimension of the self. Casanova appeals to him as the wisest man he has ever known, adding that he has taken Voltaire as his master and his father. Just before accepting his shadow, Casanova calls Voltaire "my spirit of wisdom, my best judgement."

Casanova, Voltaire, Marina and Cagliostro also serve as Hero, Philosopher-king, Mother-cum-mistress, and Magician, figures which are among the many archetypes Jung describes in the collective unconscious. But their roles as persona, self, anima and shadow are primary.

In the three charades of the second act, the characters change roles rapidly. Costumes are varied, but props are reduced to a minimum. In the second charade, Casanova and the Ideal Beloved sit side by side on two stools as if in a coach, while Voltaire sits on a table in front of them and acts as coachman. They joggle, as if travelling, and Voltaire mimes his relation to the horses. The third charade provides a lively change in mood, with Cagliostro acting first as a grotesque hag, The Charpillion's aunt, then as Toby, the trollop's hairdresser, gossip, and lover. This scene is bawdy, ribald and cruel. Amalie calls it a libel on her sex. Within the context of the entire play, this third charade is a dash of lemon which adds a desirable tartness to the piquancy of the romantic comedy.

The footman extends the range of character types and moods. Wenzel is an earthy, practical man, after the manner of many of Shakespeare's clowns. When Casanova laughs with his Beloved, after addressing her in the same romantic words used by Hugo to Amalie, Wenzel says: "Ah, get 'em giggling; everything else follows." It is Wenzel who reminds the aristrocrats that human nature is very much the same, regardless of rank. His part, as he himself calls it at the trial, is to be "the public;" or one of the speaking animals, in a situation which Amalie likens to a magical Arabian tale. It is Wenzel who interprets Cagliostro as Casanova's bad luck or Contrary Destiny. His common sense is the pinch of salt which the romance needs.

The play's title puns on the events and on the theme, since the other characters (Amalie, Hugo, Wenzel) all discover their general complicity in the sins with which Casanova is charged, and the multiple nature of their psyches. Casanova's final defence is that he has loved and revered some things truly. He is neither saint nor whimpering sinner, but an artist who has striven to give pattern to the muddle of experience: "God gave me life, and I have lived it, with the gifts and the blemishes he gave me, with as much—style, as I could."

Davies attempts the same theme of self-knowledge and integration in a later and much less successful drama, "Question Time," which played first at the Saint Lawrence Centre in Toronto in February and March, 1975. In the program notes, headed "My diary tells me that . . . ," Davies tells us that he wanted to write a play about Canada: "The theme of the play is power—what power may do to a man, and what that man in his turn does to the people around him, and to the country he leads . . . . It will appear in this play that I think Canada is gravely misshaped by its reluctance to come to terms with its inmost self and to find that inmost self in its land, which is certainly one of the oldest in the world."

Hence the setting, in the northern reaches of Canada. The entire action represents fevered fantasies in the mind of a Canadian prime minister as he lies in a coma in shock, after a plane crash. The play takes place in Les Montagnes de Glace in the distant Arctic and in the terra incognita of the Right Honourable Peter Macadam. Murray Laufer's jagged icecaps looked garish in bright light but became magical, mysterious, and romantic as the houselights dimmed—a northern baroque. The locale is intended as a place of truth, of destruction and recreation.

Macadam, son of Adam. Read *Everyman*. As in *General Confession*, the central characters are projections of the four major archetypes of the collective unconscious. Taken together, they represent the personality or psyche as Jung sees it. The *anima* is played by Macadam's wife, who describes herself as part of "the Macadam complex" composed of wife, servant and private secretary, a witty tag for a composite group who embody the various ways in which the archetypal woman is perceived by man. (Only the wife, acted with verve by Jennifer Phipps, appears in the play.) Macadam's *persona* or public mask is played by Arnak, a sprightly young woman who declares herself to be his intelligence; Macadam is known to his public as a very rational man.

A Shaman, or distinctly unorthodox Scots doctor, represents the *self*, an archetype of order and of wisdom rather than reason, who assists the personality towards integration and wholeness. Finally, the *shadow*, played here by the Leader of the Opposition, dressed in identical clothing plus a mask. This is a poor representation of the dark and frightening side of our personality with which we must come to terms. It represents Macadam's inner antagonist simply on the level of reasoned argument and political action. The Leader of the Opposition has a very slight part in the play. He has no memorable lines and does nothing to advance the Prime Minister's understanding of himself.

Anima, *persona*, *shadow*, and *self* — or those, to paraphrase Voltaire in

General Confession, without whom there could be no Peter Macadam. The P.M. calls them "strands in the fabric of my being." They exist to show him to himself from an unfamiliar point of view. One reviewer criticized the play for lacking "a central figure of any depth,"[6] but this is beside the point. The allegoric structure along Jungian lines, where the central character is represented by four or five other characters, and where he represents a nation as well as Everyman, precludes the possibility of a strong central figure. My quarrel is not with this structure, which Davies has employed to brilliant advantage in his earlier play but with the total failure of the play to present in real terms any genuine advance towards integration and maturity, either in Peter Macadam or in the nation which he represents.

The play begins with Lloyd Robertson (playing himself) on a large television screen, informing us that the Prime Minister's plane has crashed somewhere in the Arctic and that the "best medical attention available" is being sought. The scene shifts quickly to the Shaman, hamming it up in a gross parody of a witch doctor routine, as Macadam lies on a couch in a primitive shelter. In tone, the play moves easily between extremes of farce, satiric wit, and romantic comedy. This is one of its strengths. The technical device of the large television screen is also a good one, permitting, as it does, the medium to satirize itself. Since the P.M.'s spirit is invisible to the actors who do not represent parts of himself, there are amusing scenes where he stands unseen beside those who are discussing his absence or past actions.

The Shaman, more sober now, asks the P.M. whether he has any reality except in the eyes of others, and tells him that "the best of us see life through the spectacles of a temperament." Macadam's is cool and rational. The healer, reminder of the needs of the inner life, is willing to serve as guide in this unknown psychic land. The doctor is an interesting character, except for occasional truisms such as "We all pay a price for what we have and what we are." When he is asked what he *is*, the P.M. declares himself to be a creature shaped by democracy and accuses the Shaman of lacking "a modern intelligence." Arnak carries a club, since intelligence may be used as a weapon. Two amusing examples are given of the Prime Minister's witty demolishing of opponents in the House. The Shaman claims to deal with the inner world where there is a different order of reality: "The interplay between the world of fantasy and reality is what gives depth to life." When asked if he has a totem animal, the P.M. chooses the bear, thereby revealing his lack of self-knowledge. He dons the Shaman's bearskin and grovels helplessly, rolling in agony as the world rushes in through his nose. Neither this experience, nor a dramatic confrontation with his loyal wife, seems to teach Macadam anything. The first act closes with his defiance of the Shaman: "Not all wisdom lies in your primitive world, Dr. Angakok."

Act Two opens with a Mock Parliament, the Parliament of the Terra Incognita. Is the P.M. to live or die? "Defeat here is the loss of yourself."

Democracy seems to require the gelding of the hero, an idea picked up effectively towards the end of the second act, when Beaver comes onstage as a representative of Canadian diplomacy, goodwill, and appeasement. In an argument with a stronger animal, Beaver makes peace by offering up his own testicles on his broad, flat tail. Unfortunately, the sacrifice is irreversible: "When the orbs are gone, the sceptre is unavailing." Beaver is hustled out while two balls are thrown onstage, an amusing touch of slapstick.

The identification of the Prime Minister with the nation as well as with Everyman becomes explicit in the second act. Both man and country are engaged in an act of self-exploration. A Herald, a venerable and romantic figure, represents the wisdom of the past: "Nations need dreams." Why, it is asked near the end of the play, would anyone be willing to accept political power at the cost of self-estrangement? Is Peter Macadam — and Canada — simply a hollow shell?

Davies gives us no real answer to this question, only a forced or artificial one. La Sorcière des Montagnes de Glace, an ethereal figure representing the spirit of the land, "the Queen served by all earthly queens," seems to give Macadam her blessing at the end. Unfortunately, the Sorceress is more suggestive of the Fairy Queen in a high school pageant than of a genuine mystery. And the Prime Minister's recovery is *unearned*, whether one considers the personal or the national level.[7] He has chosen (acted to choose) nothing. When the Sorceress calls him child and lover, he echoes her words like a puppet. The comic ending seems to have no real justification beyond Davies' predetermined decision that his play should end happily.[8]

Davies' 1967 preface to the paperback reprint of a much earlier play, *Eros at Breakfast*(1949), attributes the origin of its form to the "health dialogues" of his primary school days. These were didactic playlets illustrating the need for cleaning one's teeth or eating good food. Davies was impressed, even as a child, by the idea of setting a scene in a human stomach. He describes *Eros at Breakfast* as "a mental health dialogue," rooted in the Freudian concept that intellectual disturbances can bring about painful physical consequences. The fact that young Mr. P.S. is composed of *four* departments, and the dramatizing of different parts of Mr. P.S. through different actors, suggests that the play is an earlier, cruder form of the Jungian theories which matured in *General Confession*. Davies still considers the setting of *Eros* the most effective part of the play.

It is springtime. The setting is a young man's Solar Plexus, depicted as a superior and luxurious departmental office. Chremes, the departmental head, addresses the audience as "distinguished psychologist," and informs them that they are looking into one of the departmental bureaus of the soul of a young fellow-townsman, Mr. P.S. The initials stand for Psyche and Soma, "Soul and Body, or Spirit and Flesh—the two substances which make him what he is."

The cast consists of five representatives of four bureaus, the Solar Plexus, the

Intelligence, the Heart and the Liver. The action and much of the humour stems from the conflicting interests and personalities of Mr. P.S.'s permanent civil service. They are reluctant, like the members of any government bureaucracy, to remember that they must work together for the good of the whole body. (Davies uses a variation of this idea in *A Masque of Aesop*, in the fable "The Belly and the Members.")

When Mr. P.S. falls in love with a young lady named Thora, all but Aristophanes of the Intelligence Department consider it an admirable state of affairs. The Jungian concept of personality as found in *The Manticore* might be considered as a very sophisticated development of this early concept of the various roles played by feeling, sentiment, and intelligence within the human body. Hepatica's description of herself as the "dash of woman" found in every proper man suggests Jung's concept of the *anima*.

Chremes' address to the members of the audience, in the manner of a polished lecturer, draws them into the action, a technique which Davies uses in his masques. Chremes tells the spectators that they are there to see something of the soul at work. Are they sceptical? "The bodily organs and the soul are more closely linked than you may imagine, however; all life is miraculous."

The disturbance introduced into Mr. P.S.'s system by his infatuation with Thora brings Aristophanes (Intellect), Parmeno (Sentiment) and eventually Hepatica (the beautiful young controller of Liver and Lights) into the Solar Plexus Department. Humour results from the tension between their opposing points of view. Parmeno admires Strauss waltzes, while Aristophanes finds them deplorable. The affair at which Mr. P.S. met Thora is a "ball" to Parmeno and a "stuffy little dance" to Aristophanes. As for the youth's attempt at poetry in honour of Thora, Parmeno terms it an outpouring of the heart; Aristophanes, "sixteen very indifferent couplets;" and Chremes, some scribbled doggerel. None of the other departments share Aristophanes' concern for Mr. P.S.'s university examinations, nor his vision of a career which proceeds from a degree through a solid financial climb to the choosing of a wife after eight or ten years of solid work.

The others suggest that Aristophanes might save face by getting drunk. Then nobody will be able to blame him for the love affair of which he disapproves. He takes their advice. The bureaucrats proceed to have a party, enlivened by Aristophanes' drunken comic songs. The contents of Thora's letter to Mr. P.S. is read over the intercom. She suggests that they go to the Dog Show together: Thora loves Airedales and seems prepared to offer the same emotion to Mr. P.S.

The play ends with Crito and Parmeno kissing Hepatica, who is worried that the audience is learning a bit too much about love — but "Who can know too much?" *Eros at Breakfast* is an amusing light comedy, and Davies is quite right: the setting is the best part.

Hunting Stuart (1955) is based upon the "romance of heredity," a phrase occurring in the Author's Note to the 1972 edition of the play. Carl Jung is never mentioned by name, as he is in Davies' recent novels, but the play is pervaded by Jungian ideas of the collective unconscious, and of the psychic baggage of ancestry which each of us carries. Davies develops the idea that our ancestral memories form a reservoir of nobility latent within us from which we can draw, if we have not allowed it to be stifled by our environment.

It is interesting to read the play in conjunction with *The Manticore* and, in particular, with the novel's climatic scene. It takes place on Christmas Eve day high up in the Swiss mountains. David Staunton is taken by Liesl Naegeli to see a prehistoric cave. Liesl is a strange devil-saint figure who embodies the Jungian concept of the shadow. The two reach the cave by crawling through a long dark passage, termed "a horrible descent." The actual journey symbolizes the passage of mankind from prehistoric times into civilization. The high-ceilinged cave is the size of a small chapel — a deliberate comparison, since this is (for Liesl, and for Davies) a religious journey. Liesl believes it to be at least seventy-five thousand years since men lived here and worshipped bears. The skulls and bones of bears are set in niches in a manner that suggests religious ritual. Liesl tells David that they share the great mysteries with their ancestors, wrestling, like them, with the facts of death and continuance. Compared with the cave, the Sistine Chapel was built yesterday: "But the purpose of both places is the same. Men sacrificed and ate of the noblest thing they could conceive, hoping to share in its virtue . . . . Does this place give you no sense of the greatness and indomitability and spiritual splendour of man? Man is a noble animal, Davey. Not a good animal; a noble animal"(p.273). David remains sceptical, unimpressed by men playing bears. He loves light and law, while Liesl can also find God in darkness.

They crawl back up through utter darkness, a terrifying journey which becomes for David an anguished, fearful striving. He reaches a point of paralysis and finds the strength to continue by remembering a nineteenth-century ancestor, a barmaid who stood in the streets of her English village and demanded money from passers-by to get herself and her bastard child to Canada. David invokes her courage and makes it back into the light. He apologizes to Liesl for his disparaging remarks and for the smallness of his understanding when he entered the cave. David wakens on Christmas day feeling renewed, reborn through the terror of the cave and Liesl's promise of love. The incident illustrates the continuity of human experience, the very real presence of our ancestors within ourselves, and the possibilities for drawing present strength out of this reservoir of experience.

The play, with its punning title, takes its characters on a hunt through time, a journey into the past which is also a journey into themselves. Two scientists arrive at the Stuart home in Ottawa with a geneological chart which shows that Henry Benedict Stuart is the last male survivor of the Stuart line, the direct descendent of Bonnie Prince Charlie. They have a powder which, when snuffed, releases memories; taken in sufficient strength, it releases ancestral memories and gives the subject the consciousness of one of his ancestors. The strength of the dose controls the time period obtained. Stuart is persuaded to become the Great Guinea Pig. Having taken the powder in a dosage calculated to move him back into the late eighteenth century, Stuart becomes Bonnie Prince Charlie, the Chevalier St. George, heir to the throne of Great Britain and Ireland. This effects a drastic personality change in him. Since the other characters are still very much themselves, the situation makes for richly comic possibilities, and Davies exploits them to the hilt. The play is a romantic comedy, a combination of qualities which is Davies' hallmark. I consider it his best, to date.

All of the characters with the exception of Stuart are caricatures or "humors," in the Jonsonian sense of being dominated by one overriding characteristic. Only Stuart is a rounded individual, and only Stuart has a sense of humour. The other characters' "humors" involve them in various foolish admirations or sacred cows. Clemmie, Stuart's aunt, reveres Positive Thinking, and the regular elimination of physical wastes, a subject she describes as being too sacred for levity. Lilian, Stuart's wife, reveres her women's club, social prestige, and her own (comically inadequate) concept of loyalty. Fred Lewis, his prospective son-in-law, has an exaggerated respect for psychology, which to Fred means the scientific observation of mankind. And Doctors Shrubsole and Sobieska, from the whimsically-entitled Coffin Foundation in New York, idolize science and the scientific method. None of these characters thinks that there is anything funny in these things. Much of Davies' humour is created from his characters' lack of it.

The play satirizes modern psychology and the scientific method, bourgeois notions of marriage (after the bedroom scene, Dr. Shrubsole remarks: "She seems to own him, body and soul"), social snobbery, women's clubs, and bureaucratic methods in the Civil Service.

The setting is the principal room in Stuart's Ottawa apartment, which consists of the top floor of an old Victorian mansion. The room serves for living, dining, and cooking. The stage directions emphasize that an inherent nobility of structure has been overlaid by fashionable vulgarity, so that the room can be hideous, pathetic, or noble as the occasion requires. The play's dominant metaphor identifies the house with its inhabitants and especially with Stuart, whose inherently noble nature is half-stifled by resignation to failure and by a domineering, small-minded wife. Lilian, with her pretentions to noble birth and her petty vanity, is responsible for the pathetic and vulgar furnishings. The daughter Caroline is denying the best in herself through her determination to be ordinary. "When you marry you get an old house over your head." This maxim becomes a refrain, used first by Lilian as she advises Carol to meet Fred's family, and later by Carol.

The action takes place on a November evening. It is continuous, the breaks between the three acts being placed so as to create amusing and dramatic suspense. The first curtain falls on a strange woman greeting Stuart as "Your Majesty!"; the second, on his retiring to the bedroom with the same strange woman while in his eighteenth-century consciousness.

Suspense is a major comic technique in this play. Throughout the first half of Act One, the audience is curious to know what horrible deed has been perpetrated by Clemmie. Lilian is "Christian-martyring" and Carol attempting to placate her, while granting that Clemmie's act is hard on her mother's social ambitions. Carol's facile sophistication contrasts amusingly with Lilian's fussiness. Clemmie arrives on the scene in the best of spirits, pleased with herself and proud of her latest business venture. Lilian's irritation increases so that by the time Stuart enters she has reached the point of trying to evict Clemmie forcibly. The audience is still ignorant of the nature of Clemmie's felony, and the struggle is the more comic for Clemmie's Positivizing, as she calls it, towards Lilian. The offending newspaper advertisement is finally read aloud. Clemmie's notoriety has been achieved by a lurid testimonial to the powers of Flush-of-Youth Tonic to cure bloating, gas, stabbing pains and faulty elimination. Suspense is also aroused when first Fred and then Stuart take the anaesthetizing powder which gives them the consciousness of one of their ancestors.

Clemmie is a delightful character, "triumphantly aspectabund," as Davies describes a comic character in Richard III.[9] Mrs. Clementina Izzard, *nee* Stolberg, is a small, stout old lady with witch-like wisps of hair and bright eyes. Her hat should suggest both an old-fashioned aristocrat and a charwoman. Her relentless good humour and high spirits contrast comically with the cold disapproval of Lilian and Carol. Clemmie's current religion is Positivity. This means that she loves everyone, especially her enemies (read *Lilian*). Clemmie thinks of herself as a Power-House of Positivity. When Lilian, goaded beyond endurance, attempts to pull her out of her chair, Clemmie sits with eyes shut and teeth clenched saying cheerfully that love is stronger than hate. Lilian has an inflated ideal of service which Clemmie matches: being "called" to serve people by recommending patent medicines to them makes her a Positive Force.

As in *At the Gates of the Righteous*, Davies uses one type of cant as a foil for another type, so that the ridiculousness of both types is clear to the spectators while the characters persist in seeing only the folly of the other, not their own. Lil's ambition is to play a part in what she calls "the world of active, thinking, vital women who are spreading their influence everywhere, and making themselves felt in the councils of the nation." Clemmie's language is earthy, her point of view ruthless in connection with Lilian's social climbing. She calls Lilian a "negativizing snob," and her friends, "gas-bags." This does not prevent Clemmie from using a high-flying rhetoric in her role as the Flush-of-Youth Lady. Davies uses the opposing rhetorics of Bill Balmer and young Fingal in a similar way in the earlier play.

Clemmie's role is less prominent after the first act. She hides when the scientists arrive, afraid that they have come from the Medical Association to charge her with fraud. (One of the childless Clemmie's testimonials began ''After the baby came.'') Her head bobs up farcically from time to time over the kitchen counter as events interest her. Her enthusiasm for the scientific experiment contrasts with Lilian's scepticism, and her reverence for Stuart, be he Bonnie Prince Charlie or simply her nephew, contrasts with the latter's disrespect.

This reverential love is connected with the dramatic healing of Clemmie's arthritic hand in the last scene. Stuart's last act as king is the exercise of the Royal Touch. This is a deeply moving scene, one which reminds us of the depth of meaning of the monarchy. The candlelight hides the trumpery decor and reveals the nobility of the old house. Stuart regards his elderly nurse with compassion and love. Beside an improvised altar, while Fred reads from the majestic Twenty-First Psalm, depicting the king as the servant of the Lord, Stuart touches Clemmie's gnarled hand. As Fred concludes the psalm, Clemmie raises her hand, now straight and firm.

Stuart's original entry, while his wife is wrestling with his aunt, is effective comedy. Earlier, Carol has told Lilian that her father's students are all aware of his sex appeal. Stuart is directed to be a dark, handsome man who would be distinguished were he not content to play second fiddle to everyone. He later describes himself as a failure, a man without much indignation but with a talent for happiness. Stuart announces that he has been promoted to Number One C.I.P., a comic title standing for Correspondence in Pendency. His job parodies paper-pushing, paper proliferation and procrastination in a bureaucracy. Clemmie matches this good news by telling of her advertising contract. Lilian was to read a paper to her women's club that evening on ''Some Local Pioneer Families Connected with the Nobility and Gentry of Great Britain'' (her own family included, we suspect). She had hoped to get on the National Executive but now may have to resign.

Carol's overly serious young suitor Fred is described as being too full of green knowledge to have any sense of humour. It is Fred who analyzes Clemmie's crime. Our society, he says, thinks of laxatives with a complex of humour and abhorrence, fear and desire.[10] Fred's idea of an ideal marriage is a temporary arrangement between rational parties based upon psychoanalysis. He scorns heredity, while acknowledging the importance of environment. Fred's ideas, which include the superiority of reason to feeling, are gently debunked. After taking the drug, Fred becomes a glib spokesman for phrenology, the psychological science most admired at the time (1855). He acts like a sideshow barker, while his sentimental rhetoric barely disguises his lecherous intentions towards Carol. Today's scientist may be tomorrow's quack. Carol and Fred are several degrees wiser at the end of the play, and we enjoy their conversion.

Stuart's change from a henpecked, cautious husband into a haughty, roistering aristocrat is the heart of the comedy. As Bonnie Prince Charlie, Stuart bullies his mistress Walkinshaw (Lilian is reluctantly conscripted into this part) yet is also tender towards her. He describes Walkinshaw as "an honest trollop, except at cards," and prepares to play for her housekeeping money. One of the funniest scenes involves Lil's fellow clubwoman's telephone call and a three-way conversation between a distracted Lilian, a drunken Stuart (as The Chevalier), and the squawking phone voices. The conversion, however, has its serious side. One aspect of this is man's need for dignity and respect. As Shrubsole reminds Lilian, every man is a king, and if no one will acknowledge it, he dies; she should "secure and cherish the moment of kingship."

Dr. Sobieska's admiration for the Chevalier is more than reciprocated after Stuart has taken the drug. He carries his handsome "cousin" off to the bedroom. Dr. Shrubsole, Sobieska's husband, takes the situation with admirable calmness. If he has to be cuckolded, better it should be by a man who died, "for all official purposes," in 1788. His advice to Lilian to consider herself a martyr to science, worthy of a footnote when the experiment is written, does little to allay her hysteria. She considers sexual infidelity "the one unforgivable thing." Shrubsole's confidence that his wife has the experiment under control proves to be correct. There is a crash and a masculine shout from the bedroom, whereupon Clemmie is called to attend upon Stuart's slight contusion. Sobieska calms her jealous husband with assurances that what passed in the bedroom was simply scientific "fieldwork."

The play leaves Stuart clothed in his twentieth-century consciousness but with a new attitude, in the manner of David Staunton in *The Manticore*. The nobility of the old house is revealed by moonlight in the last scene. Stuart phones to book a flight to Scotland, presumably to begin a hunt for his ancestors which is also a hunt for self-knowledge and wholeness, the goal of life in Jungian terms. While ambiguous, the ending clearly hints that Stuart will no longer be "a kind of prisoner" to a petty job and a domineering wife.

Jung's concept of the collective unconscious underlies Dr. Sobieska's admonition to Caroline: "Perhaps 'now' is a little bigger than you suspect." *Now* is as big as man's collective past.[11] Heredity is the old house over everyone's head. Carol and Lilian dislike and fear the experiment and its implications, whereas Clemmie welcomes it. It hasn't surprised her at all, she tells Lilian. Just confirmed her intuitions. And what fun it is! "All of a sudden life stops being gray and messy, and gets bright-coloured and exciting." What else would one expect from the Comedy Company of the Psyche?

Notes to Chapter 6

1. See Calvin S. Hall and Vernon J. Nordby, *A Primer of Jungian Psychology* (New York: Mentor Book, New American Library, 1973), pp.41-42.

2. See James Joyce, *Ulysses* (London: Bodley Head,1964), p.646.

3. John A. Sanford, *Dreams, God's Forgotten Language* (Philadelphia: Lippincott, 1968), p.130.

4. When Jung was a university student, a strange incident took place in his home. A large bread knife, lying in a basket, suddenly shattered into several pieces. A cutler pronounced the pieces to be sound and said that someone must have deliberately broken the knife. Years later, when Jung's wife was fatally ill, Jung took the pieces from his safe and had them mounted as a whole knife. See Hall and Nordby, *A Primer of Jungian Psychology*, p.21. This incident from Jung's life seems to be suggested in Davies' symbol for the breaking of the shadow's antagonism.

5. Carl Jung, *Two Essays on Analytical Psychology*, Collected Works, Vol.7 (Princeton: Princeton University Press), 238.

6. Urjo Kareda, "Question Time is a grand disaster," *Toronto Star*, 26 February 1975, p.E20.

7. Cf. Scott Young, "Hero gelding," *Globe and Mail*, 28 February 1975, p.27: "But in my view he does need to show some dimension backward into what he was that was so great that a play should be devoted with great skill, fun and humanity toward his rediscovery of his own true worth."

8. See also Herbert Whittaker, "Question Time complex and glittering," *Globe and Mail*, 26 February 1975, p.14:"What Davies has produced, at the peak of his literary success, is a morality drama for our time, thrusting at an awakening public yet another aspect of its nationalism." Whittaker finds the play to be an unqualified success, whereas Urjo Kareda, *op. cit.*, calls it "a very grand, ambitious and idiosyncratic disaster of the order that only Robertson Davies could have created . . . a failure with a master's signature on it."

9. Davies takes the word from an eighteenth-century critic who used it to denote the true comedian's ability to look comical even when he is not speaking. See Robertson Davies and Tyrone Guthrie, *Renown at Stratford. A Record of the Shakespearean Festival in Canada* (Toronto: Clarke, Irwin, 1953), p.66.

10. The fanaticism of an earlier generation of Canadians on the subject of laxatives comes into both *Fifth Business* and *The Manticore*. Michael Bliss in "'Pure Books on Avoided Subjects': Pre-Freudian Sexual Ideas in Canada," an hilarious article delivered to the Canadian Historical Association in 1970, shows that regular elimination was valued by an earlier generation of Canadians as a means of reducing the "stress of sexual impulse" and hence of sexual excess.

11. See "Acta Interviews Robertson Davies," *Acta Victoriana*, Vol. XCVII, No. 2 (April, 1973), p.83: "Jung's analyses . . . attempted to relate the patient to the whole world, not only the world in which he lived but the world of the imagination, the world of myths, legends, humanity, mankind." See also pp. 82-84, where Davies describes Jung's influence on his thought.

'Through scorn, to love'

Davies' Apollo, in his *Masque of Aesop*, speaks of the greatest teacher as the one who has passed through scorn of mankind to love of mankind. Marchbanks may rest in scorn. But the larger work of his creator exhibits the love of country and of his fellow man of which the fictional Apollo speaks.

Davies has been called the Bernard Shaw of the Canadian theatre, although the same critic thinks that Davies does not share Shaw's passion for social reform.[1] Davies' plays do contain social criticism. To support this claim one has only to think of the attacks on popular educational and psychological doctrines or on philistine neglect of art in *Fortune, My Foe*; the burlesque of conflicting social attitudes in *At the Gates of the Righteous*; or the mockery of materialism and of popular cynicism in his two masques.

For over thirty years, moreover, Davies' work has exhibited a concern for the relationship between the artist and his society. The social thrust behind his themes demands that we ask ourselves what art is, why people need it, how a society encourages or discourages it, and what makes a society great. The symbiotic relationship between the artist and his culture is one of Davies' recurring concerns.

It is also true, however, that Davies' drama is by no means purely concerned with social reform, nor does he believe in preaching. He aspires, by his own admission, to record the bizarre and passionate life of the Canadian people.[2]

In 1951, in an article prepared for the Royal Commission on National Development in the Arts, Letters and Sciences, Davies defined the theatre as the Temple of Passions and as a compost of many arts; eleven years later, he calls it a temple of feeling, where dreams and wishes are paramount.[3] His idea of theatre, then, does not seem to have changed during the period in which he wrote his chief plays. He speaks, in 1951, of the sense of exhilaration and fulfillment which first-rate theatre can give; of its vulgarity (one thinks, here, of Mr. Punch); and of the importance to it of tradition: "the theatre is a vigorous, living, and in a certain sense, a coarse art; it is vulgar in the true sense of the word''; ''and the theatre, perhaps more than the other arts, relies upon a living tradition.''[4] He adds that the stage can give us ''a sense of the wonder and nearness of the great past.'' Certainly Davies manages to do this in *Hunting Stuart*. He describes the theatre as educational and recreative, but not primarily so. People who try to use it as social medicine (as do Mattie and Orville in *Fortune*) will kill it. Theatre is an art and, above all, a craft:

> *One must consider the actors, and give them opportunities to show their own special skill as distinguished from your own. One must know how to build up a speech to a climax, and then how to get down from the climax without tumbling. One must not introduce characters who do not help to carry forward the story, for actors cost money and must not be wasted. And above all, one must beware of the wrong kind of subtlety, for the delicate shades which give distinction to a novel have no place in a play: the subtlety of the playwright lies in quite another direction—not less than the novelist's, but different.*[5]

In the 1951 article, as in his plays (especially *Hope Deferred*), Davies reiterates that for a nation to be great, it must have a great art. His suggestions at that time included a recommendation to establish a practical theatre studio in Canada, modelled upon the Old Vic Theatre Centre in London, England.

From such a theoretical base, it is not surprising that Davies' drama should be both romantic and, in the best sense, melodramatic. Oxford defines melodrama as a theatrical piece with a happy ending, one characterized by sensational incident and by violent appeals to the emotions. Davies links it with other forms of drama through its concern to make dreams manifest.[6] Melodrama is despised, he notes, by those who see drama, erroneously, as the younger sister of literature. Melodrama may provide a great actor with the scaffold on which to hang ''a personal creation of extraordinary psychological power . . . . There is more in melodrama than a solely literary approach can reveal.''[7] James Reaney, who has often gone on record in defence of melodrama, would agree. Davies describes his play *General Confession* as being written in the ''guise'' of nineteenth-century melodrama.

What might be surprising — although it should not be so to those who are familiar with Canadian writing — is the combination of irony with melodrama and romance. That thoroughly Canadian combination may be seen in the work of a nineteenth-century writer like James de Mille (in his intriguing anti-Utopian fiction, *A Strange Manuscript Found in a Copper Cylinder*) or of a modern such as Leonard Cohen. Certainly it may be seen in Davies' work, which often presents a romantic situation from an ironic point of view. The irony is part of an overall urbanity which reflects a sophisticated and cultured mind. James Noonan writes that Davies' plays demonstrate ''brilliance in theatricality and dialogue that is unmatched by any of our playwrights today.''[8]

This urbanity is part of everything Davies writes, whether it be about the eccentricities of book collectors or the difficulties and joys of staging a Gilbert and Sullivan operetta.

Peter Newman has described Davies as an artist who has always found Canada "hard to endure if impossible to flee."[9] Davies told Newman that it is spiritual suicide to divorce yourself from your roots: "A lot of people complain that my novels aren't about Canada. I think they are, because I see Canada as a country torn between a very northern, rather extraordinary mystical spirit which it fears and its desire to present itself to the world as a Scotch banker. This makes for tension. Tension is the very stuff of art. Plays, novels — the whole lot."[10] Both to Newman and in "The Poetry of a People," Davies speaks of our national shadow (in Jungian terms) as being our habit of repressing emotion.[11] Canadians feel deeply, but are ashamed of their feelings and attempt to conceal them. Davies sees Canadian writings as being marked by stern strength, passionate but controlled feeling, and irony: "Only our travel posters are painted in primary colours; our history and our temperament use a darker palette."[12] In Jungian theory, an individual must come to terms with his shadow to achieve maturity. Perhaps Davies' indulgence of his Celtic intuition and emotion is his way of countering Canadian reticence and the repression of emotion.

Let us not forget, finally, that Davies writes comedies. And comedies have happy endings. They are concerned with joy, and with freedom. So is Davies. In his *Notes on the New Theatre* (Stratford Festival Souvenir Program, 1957), Davies speaks of the optimistic quality of the Stratford venture, in the archaic (1795) sense which Oxford Dictionary gives for optimism:"the character or quality of being for the best." It is an attitude which faces difficulties squarely but looks beyond them, an attitude which typifies not only Stratford in Canada but also the vision out of which Davies writes. Have we the courage to see ourselves as funny people, Davies asks in his 1962 essay on theatre? I would say that we have, and we have the comic artists to prove it. Davies speaks, in his Introduction to Leacock's *Moonbeams from the Larger Lunacy*, of the magical spirit of fun; or, again, of "the comic glory of laughter."[13] He quotes approvingly, in his Introduction to *Renown at Stratford*, from Chesterton's description of great comedy as the mysticism of happiness. These phrases reflect the importance of humour and its intimate connection with the human spirit.

Davies has recently written of the importance of curiosity, which he describes as one of the greatest and most life-enhancing of human qualities, one without which no life has any savor or great meaning.[14] Once again, the reader senses a maturing vision which is still very much of a piece with its earlier form. In 1962, in a speech at Queen's University Convocation on the occasion of receiving an honorary doctorate, Davies warned students against *acedie* or sloth, a spiritual and intellectual torpor which represents a failure in the art of living and which is the only kind of failure that really breaks the spirit. One can be superficially busy and still be a victim of this crippling indifference which was reckoned by medieval theologians as one of the seven deadly sins. Hence Davies' advice to take care that feeling is not neglected, and to cultivate joy: "We live in a world where too many people are pitifully afraid of joy. Because I wish you well, I beg you not to add yourself to their number."

Davies' drama celebrates feelings, feelings both painful and happy. It takes us through "Fruitful irrationality"[15] and the "fruitful unconscious"[16] towards a Promised Land governed by Joy.

Notes to Chapter 7

1. See James Noonan, review of *Hunting Stuart and Other Plays*, *Queen's Quarterly*, LXXX, 3 (Autumn, 1973), p.467.

2. See Donald Cameron, *Conversations with Canadian Novelists*, Part One (Toronto: Macmillan, 1973), p. 38.

3. See Robertson Davies, "The Theatre. A Dialogue on the State of the Theatre in Canada," *Royal Commission Studies: A Selection of Essays Prepared for the Royal Commission on National Development in the Arts, Letters and Sciences* (Ottawa: King's Printer, 1951), p. 370; and "The Theatre," in D.C. Williams, ed., *The Arts as Communication* (Toronto: University of Toronto Press, 1962), p. 22.

4. Davies, "The Theatre. A Dialogue on the State of the Theatre in Canada," pp. 372, 374.

5. Ibid, pp. 387-388.

6. See Robertson Davies, "Letters in Canada:1965," *University of Toronto Quarterly*, XXXV, 4 (July, 1966), 415.

7. Ibid.

8. James Noonan, review of *Hunting Stuart*, p. 466.

9. Peter C. Newman, "The Master's Voice," *Maclean's* (September, 1972), p. 42.

10. Ibid, p. 43.

11. See A. Wainwright, ed., *Notes for a Native Land* (Ottawa: Oberon Press, 1969), p.98.

12. Robertson Davies, "The Northern Muse," *Holiday*, 35, 4 (April, 1964), 10.

13. Davies, "A Dialogue on the State of the Theatre in Canada," p. 378.

14. Robertson Davies, "Curiosity, work open the door to life's splendor," *The Globe and Mail*, 9 November 1974, p. 7.

15. Robertson Davies, "The Heart of a Merry Christmas," Address to the Canadian Club, Toronto, 14 December 1970.

16. Robertson Davies, "Letters in Canada: 1965," p. 416.

BIBLIOGRAPHY

ROBERTSON DAVIES

Plays:
Eros at Breakfast and Other Plays, intro. Tyrone Guthrie.
Toronto: Clarke, Irwin, 1949. This collection contains *Eros at Breakfast*, *The Voice of the People, Hope Deferred, Overlaid* and *At the Gates of the Righteous.*
Fortune, My Foe. Toronto: Clarke, Irwin, 1949.
At My Heart's Core. Toronto: Clarke, Irwin, 1950.
A Masque of Aesop. Toronto: Clarke, Irwin, 1952.
A Jig for the Gypsy. Toronto: Clarke, Irwin, 1954.
A Masque of Mr. Punch. Toronto: Oxford University Press, 1963.
Four Favorite Plays. Toronto: Clarke, Irwin, 1968 (rpt.). This collection contains *Eros at Breakfast*, *The Voice of the People*, *At the Gates of the Righteous*, and *Fortune My Foe.*
Hunting Stuart and Other Plays. Toronto: New Press, 1972. This collection contains *Hunting Stuart*, *King Phoenix*, and *General Confession.*
"Leaven of Malice," performed in 1973 at Hart House Theatre, Toronto and in 1975 at Niagara-on-the-Lake (unpublished).
"Brothers in the Black Art," performed on CBC television 14 Feb. 1974, Executive Producer Fletcher Markel.
"The Centennial Play," performed in Lindsay 1966, and in Ottawa (as revised by Peter Boretski) in 1967.
Question Time. Toronto: Macmillan, 1975.

Fiction:
The Diary of Samuel Marchbanks. Toronto: Clarke, Irwin, 1947.
The Table Talk of Samuel Marchbanks. Toronto: Clarke, Irwin, 1949.
Samuel Marchbanks' Almanack. Toronto: McClelland & Stewart, 1967; NCL ed. 1968, Intro. Gordon Roper.
Tempest-Tost. Toronto: Clarke, Irwin, 1951; paperback rpt. 1965.
Leaven of Malice. Toronto: Clarke, Irwin, 1954; paperback rpt. 1964.
A Mixture of Frailties. Toronto: Macmillan, 1958; paperback rpt. 1968.
Fifth Business. Toronto: Macmillan, 1970; Signet paperback, 1971.
The Manticore. Toronto: Macmillan, 1972.
World of Wonders. Toronto: Macmillan, 1975.

Non-fiction:
Shakespeare's Boy Actors. London: Dent, 1939.
Shakespeare for Young Players. Toronto: Clarke, Irwin, 1942.

A Voice from the Attic. Toronto: McClelland & Stewart, 1960 (published in England as *The Personal Art*. London: Secker and Warburg, 1961).

Feast of Stephen (anthology). Toronto: McClelland & Stewart, 1970 (long introduction separately published as *Stephen Leacock*, Canadian Writers Series, McClelland & Stewart, 1970).

In collaboration with Sir Tyrone Guthrie:

Renown at Stratford. Toronto: Clarke, Irwin, 1953; 1971.

Twice Have the Trumpets Sounded. Toronto: Clarke, Irwin, 1954.

Thrice the Brinded Cat Hath Mew'd. Toronto: Clarke, Irwin, 1955.

Selected articles:

"Remember Creatore," *Mayfair Magazine* (September, 1948), pp.59-60.

"Three worlds, three summers — but not the summer just past," *Mayfair Magazine*, XXX (September, 1949), pp.58, 86-92.

"The Theatre. A Dialogue on the State of the Theatre in Canada," *Royal Commission Studies: A Selection of Essays Prepared for the Royal Commission on National Development in the Arts, Letters and Sciences* (1949-1951). Ottawa: The King's Printer, 1951, pp. 369-392.

"The Genius of Dr. Guthrie," *Theatre Arts*, XL, 3 (March, 1956), 28-29,90.

"Stephen Leacock," *Our Living Tradition. Seven Canadians*, ed. Claude Bissell. Toronto: University of Toronto Press, in association with Carleton University, 1957, pp.128-149. *Notes on the New Theatre*. Stratford Festival Souvenir Program, 1957.

"Party of One: The Northern Muse," *Holiday*, 35, 4(April, 1964), 10-21.

"The Theatre," *The Arts as Communication*, ed. D.C. Williams, Toronto: University of Toronto Press, 1962, pp.17-31.

Review of *Tragedy* by Sidney Lamb, *Three Restoration Comedies* ed. by G.G. Falle, and *Eighteenth Century Tragedy* and *Hiss the Villain* by Michael Booth, *University of Toronto Quarterly*, XXXV, 4 (July, 1966), in "Letters in Canada 1965," 414-416.

"Letters: The Unfashionable Canadians," *Century. 1867-1967. The Canadian Saga*, ed. John D. Harbron. Toronto: Southam Press, 1967, pp.54-55.

"The Poetry of a People," *Notes for a Native Land*, ed. Andy Wainwright. Ottawa: Oberon Press, 1969, pp.96-99.

"Leacock as a Literary Artist," *Varsity Graduate*, III, 4(Winter, 1970-71), 78-87.

"Ben Jonson and Alchemy," *Stratford Papers* 1968-69, ed. B.A.W. Jackson. Hamilton: McMaster University Library Press, 1972, pp.40-60.

SELECTED CRITICISM ON DAVIES:

Anon. "Acta Interviews Robertson Davies," *Acta Victoriana*, XCVII, 2(April, 1973), 68-87.

Anon. "The Myth and the Master," *Time* (3 November, 1975), pp.8-12.

Buitenhuis, Elspeth. *Robertson Davies*. Canadian Writers and Their Works Series. Toronto: Forum House, 1972.

Cameron, Donald. "Robertson Davies: The Bizarre and Passionate Life of the Canadian People," *Conversations with Canadian Novelists*, Part One. Toronto: Macmillan, 1973, pp.30-48.

Cohen, Nathan. "Theatre Today: English Canada," *Tamarack Review*, 13 (Autumn, 1959), pp.24-37.

Knelman, Martin. "The masterful actor who plays Robertson Davies," *Saturday Night* (June, 1975), pp.30-35.

McPherson, Hugo. "The Mask of Satire: Character and Symbolic Pattern in Robertson Davies' Fiction," *Canadian Literature*, 4 (Spring, 1960), pp.18-30.

Moore, Mavor. *Four Canadian Playwrights: Robertson Davies, Gratien Gélinas, James Reaney, George Ryga*. Toronto: Holt, Rinehart & Winston of Canada, 1973. See Foreword, Background, and chapter on Robertson Davies.

Newman, Peter. "The Master's Voice. The Table Talk of Robertson Davies," *Maclean's* (September, 1972), pp.42-43.

Noonan, James. Review of *Hunting Stuart and Other Plays, Queen's Quarterly*, LXXX, 3(Autumn, 1973), 466-468.

Owen, Ivon. "The Salterton Novels," *Tamarack Review*, IX (Autumn, 1958), pp.56-63.

Roper, Gordon. "Robertson Davies' *Fifth Business* and 'that old fantastical duke of dark corners, C.G. Jung,'" *Journal of Canadian Fiction*, I,1(Winter, 1972), 33-39 (from his forthcoming book on Robertson Davies).

Scott, Patrick. "Public is behind Robertson Davies even if the literary mafia is not," *Toronto Star*, 3 Feb. 1973, p. 81.

Solly, William. "Nothing Sacred. Humour in Canadian Drama in English," *Canadian Literature*, 11 (Winter, 1962), pp.14-27.

Steinberg, M.W. "Don Quixote and the Puppets: Theme and Structure in Robertson Davies' Drama," *Canadian Literature*, 7 (Winter, 1961), pp.45-53.

Vineberg, Dusty. "Devil's Advocate," *Montreal Star*, 3 Feb. 1973, p. C7.

West, Paul. "Sluices of Literacy," review of *The Arts as Communication*, *Canadian Literature*, 14 (Autumn, 1962), 62-64.

BIBLIOGRAPHIES

Ball, J.L., compiler. "A Bibliography of Theatre History in Canada, 1606-1959," *Canadian Literature*, 14 (Autumn, 1962), pp.85-100.

Cummings, Richard, *et al*, eds. *The Brock Bibliography of Published Canadian Stage Plays in English 1900-1972* (annotated). St. Catherines: Brock University, 1972.

Index

Apuleius, 14
Arnold, Matthew, 1

At My Heart's Core, 12,21-24
At the Gates of the Righteous, 15,26-28,61,65

Becket, Samuel, 47
Boretski, Peter, 3
Brecht, Bertolt, 47
"Brothers in the Black Art," 3,26,34-37

Cameron, Donald, 9
"Centeniial Play, The," 3-4
Cervantes, Miguel, 13
Chesterton, G.K., 67
Cohen, Leonard, 66
Cohen, Nathan, 5
Crest Theatre, 5

Dominion Drama Festival, 5,10

Eliot, T.S., 39,46
Eros at Breakfast, 1,2,3,7,44,57-58

Fifth Business, 2,4,5,9,36
Fortune My Foe, 5,8,9,10,12-17,18,24,28,65
Freudian theory, 2,47

General Confession, 2,4,6,50-55,56,66
Gilbert and Sullivan operettas, 8
Guthrie, Tyrone, 2,3,4,5,7,8,17

Hart House Theatre, 3,5
Heavysege, Charles, 5,39
Hope Deferred, 12,17-19,66
Hunting Stuart, 2,3,4,6,58-63,66

International Players of Kingston, 5

Japanese Theatre, 38
Jig for the Gypsy, A, 26,31-34
Jones, Inigo, 42
Jonson, Ben, 42-43,45
Joyce, James, 8,53
Jung, Carl, 2,50
Jungian theory, 2,4,50,52-53,54,55,57,58-59,63,67

King Phoenix, 26,28-31,32

Langham, Michael, 5
Laurence, Margaret, 37
Leacock medal for humour, 10
Leacock, Stephen, 1,67
Leaven of Malice, 3
"Leaven of Malice," 3,26,37-40
Leech, Clifford, 9

Macdonald, Grant, 13
MacLennan, Hugh, 20
Mair, Charles, 5
Major, Leon, 3
Manticore, The, 2,4,10,43,50,58,59,63
Marceau, Marcel, 38
Marchbanks, Samuel, 7,9,10
Markel, Fletcher, 34
Marlowe, Christopher, 48
masque, 8,42-43,48,51,58,65
Masque of Aesop,A, 43-45,58,65
Masque of Mr. Punch,A, 8,39,45-48
Massey College, 9
Mille, James de, 66
Mitchell, W.O., 3
Mixture of Frailties, A, 4,12,17,19,34
Molière, 17,18
Moore, Mavor, 5,12
Murphy, Arthur, 3

Newman, Peter, 66
New Play Society, 5
Nicol, Eric, 3
Noonan, James, 66

Oedipus, 37,39
Orgel, Stephen, 42
Overlaid 12,19-20

Peterborough Examiner, The, 9
Philistines, the, 1
Puritanism, 20

Question Time, 4,55-57

Reaney, James, 66
Ruskin, John, 32,33

Salterton trilogy, 4,12,34,45
Sanford, John, 53
Sartre, Jean Paul, 47
Shakespearean Festival, 2,4,5,67
Shaw, G. Bernard, 3,26,40,65
Sidney, Sir Philip, 4
Stratford: *see* Shakespearean Festival
Sutherland, Arthur, 12

Tempest-Tost, 4,17
Thamesville, 7
Theatre of the Absurb, The, 47
Theriault, Yves, 3

Voice of the People, The, 12,20-21

World of Wonders, 4